DEBT OF HONOUR

DEBT
OF
HONOUR

The Story of the
International League for the
Protection of Horses

JEREMY JAMES

MACMILLAN

LONDON

First published 1994 by Macmillan London

a division of Pan Macmillan Publishers Ltd
Cavaye Place London SW10 9PG
and Basingstoke

Associated companies throughout the world

ISBN 00 333 61791 6

1 3 5 7 9 8 6 4 2

A CIP catalogue record for this book is available from
the British Library

Photoset by Parker Typesetting Service, Leicester
Printed and bound in Great Britain by
Mackays of Chatham plc, Chatham, Kent

CONTENTS

ACKNOWLEDGEMENTS

When Colonel George Stephen commissioned me to write this book, I had little idea of what I was letting myself in for.

I had not expected to find myself standing beside a tank in the destroyed town of Lipik in Croatia looking over the broken remains of a Lippizaner stud. I had not expected to find myself in the hold of a cargo vessel with a thousand horses destined for slaughter in the abattoirs of Italy; nor had I realized then the powerful emotions both those events would raise in me. I had not expected to be in the rubbish dumps of Mexico City with the WTFE farriers, nor find myself in the airless, donkey-braying souks of Morocco.

No, I had not anticipated those things.

So, first of all I would like to thank George Stephen.

I would like to thank you, George, for the commission and the great privilege of writing this book.

It has been an extraordinary experience and there has been much to write about.

Sometimes, though, I have been stuck for what to cut out and what to include and so necessarily there are omissions. I have tried to cover as broad a canvas as I can and tell the story in its entirety, through the lightness of its anecdotes to the moments of its gravity. I have tried to include many who work within the organization today while not missing out all those whose names have been closely associated with it in the past. But I have not been able to include everyone fully nor follow up on every story. It has been hard to decide. And I am conscious sometimes, perhaps, of making the wrong decisions.

For this I apologize now.

I have been helped all the way along the line. I have been helped by the office staff of the ILPH, particularly Sarah Bligh and Tricia Horne, Lucinda Barnes, Heather Stephen, Jane Gale and Liz Hatton. I have been helped by Richard Felton, and Sue Blackett, Pat Smith, and Pat Williams, and Sarah White, Sarah Gould, Nikki Smith, Kay Watson, by Maggs Harris and Anne

Gibbons, Polly Morton and Christine Thomas, by Shona Kirk, Janet Adcock, Jack and Carrie Ritson, by Mick and Jane Elwick, by Shane Morely, Denise Sharman and Leslie Southward.

I have been helped by members of the Council, by the Chairman Norman McLeod and by Jean McDougall, Alan Colvin, Dennis Beresford, Angus Panton, Noel Carding and Jeanette Butcher, and if you do not recognize what help you might have given me, all I can say is that even the quickest and most insignificant remark can sometimes throw a beam of light into a fellow's darkness and only I know who said what and when and how enormously helpful it has been.

Thanks too, Roderick Watt, for your guidance on legal matters.

The grooms of the ILPH have helped too: not only by chatting but by their kindness in looking after my horses while I was researching this book – they got kicked and bitten by my Romanian mare and run away with by my Criollo gelding and trodden on by my fat Bulgarian Nonius, Karo. They even put up with the ravages of my revolting old mutt.

To each of you I offer, with sincerity, my thanks.

To have worked with you all has been a great pleasure.

I have a lot of members of the ILPH to thank too, and I would like to say how impressed I have been by their loyalty.

The field officers – particularly Norman Brown, Ray Jackson, Tony Schormann and Ron Jordan – have been a fund of information. I would like to have spent more time with the field officers: theirs is a story all of its own.

Thanks Hamish Lochore and Eileen Gillen, and all of you in Belwade. Thanks too to Ian Gibbs of Cherry Tree Farm.

And, although I might never see them again, I would like to thank the farriers and vets of Mexico and Morocco, and Jacques Le Marquis in France, and Jean Peloux, inspector on the ships that cross the Atlantic carrying horses. And lastly (as you will have seen, this stands in no order of preference), thanks Walt Taylor and Tina MacGregor, and your extraordinarily potent Working Together For Equines team, even though you've got my old chum and master saddler, André Bubear, working with you.

Here then, is the story of the ILPH. And if I see it as you, my reader, do not, then the fault lies with me: any mistakes and misunderstandings are mine also.

I am very pleased that the publication of the story of the International League for the Protection of Horses should coincide with my Presidency. I have watched the work of the ILPH with great interest recently and have grown to appreciate how much it has done for the genuine welfare of the horse.

In the ILPH we have a pragmatic organization, that thinks through the real dangers to our horses in this increasingly over-crowded age of the internal combustion engine. It encourages the use and not the abuse of the horse, recognizing that the only hope for the future of this unique animal, particularly in the Western World, is in the pleasure it can give in sport and leisure in a rural environment.

The ILPH is a caring but not a sentimental body. From its earliest days it has emphasized that horses should work closely with mankind, believing that both benefit greatly from the partnership. This is well demonstrated in its recent work with Riding for the Disabled. Using horses who have been disadvantaged in their lives, to help people who are disadvantaged, must be a sensible use of horse power.

It also does a great deal of work in the area of education worldwide. The story of its Working Together for Equines scheme is well told in this book. Already hundreds of farriers and saddlers in many countries have been taught to help themselves. They in their turn are passing on these lessons, which bring relief to working horses, donkeys and mules in developing countries. The future expansion is endless.

This book is a worthy tribute to the ILPH and to its founder, the redoubtable Ada Cole who started it all in 1927. It is an exciting and interesting story, told with humour and sympathy. Above all it is a story of optimism, for the survival of our horses in the modern world. It is a story with a future.

Anne

. . . And then, that evening
Late in the summer the strange horses came.
We heard a distant tapping on the road,
A deepening drumming; it stopped, went on again
And at the corner changed to hollow thunder.
We saw the heads
Like a wild wave charging and were afraid.
We had sold our horses in our fathers' time
To buy new tractors. Now they were strange to us
As fabulous steeds set on an ancient shield
Or illustrations in a book of knights.
We did not dare go near them. Yet they waited,
Stubborn and shy, as if they had been sent
By an old command to find our whereabouts
And that long-lost archaic companionship.
In the first moment we had never a thought
That they were creatures to be owned and used.
Among them were some half-a-dozen colts,
Dropped in some wilderness of the broken world,
Yet new as if they had come from their own Eden.
Since then they have pulled our ploughs and borne our loads,
But that free servitude still can pierce our hearts.
Our life is changed; their coming our beginning.

EDWIN MUIR, *The Horses*

PROLOGUE

San Francisco Hacienda lies at the smart end of town on the outskirts of Mexico City. It's a replica of a Spanish Empire homestead; big, low-lying and airy.

You drive to it through the labyrinth of up-town suburbia and enter it through an arch that is flanked by a pair of tall sun-bleached studded oak doors. To the left and right of the wide gravel car park are paddocks and a tennis court, while the main hacienda buildings stand straight ahead; squat, whitewashed buildings with red pantile roofs, lime coinstones, and windows with ornate wrought-iron bow-grills over them.

The buildings surround a courtyard which is shaded by gums, acacias and jacarandas, and edging the courtyard are flower beds full of strelitzia and gladioli and hibiscus.

To one side stands a line of pillars which front the stables in a long wide verandah where grooms tend the horses or clean tack or polish boots.

Below the stables and hacienda buildings on a couple of terraces were the riding manèges, and when we arrived a girl was free-lunging a big bay Thoroughbred–Quarter Horse cross round a small ring, trying to get him to steady his paces for jumping. He was sleek and glossy and under the sunlight his coat shimmered with a metallic sheen.

The girl was working him hard. She went on working him hard until he was hot and sweaty, pushing him round until he became irritated; but still she pushed him.

She was joined in her work by her groom, a man with a huge belly and side whiskers, and that horse didn't much like him. He snorted and tensed and pulled his ears back and flicked his tail at him and you could tell that man had done something to that horse and the horse hadn't forgotten.

Casually watching this performance were a few young men who

1

were slouching around on white metal chairs and tables in the shade of the trees. They were smoking and watching the girl and the fat man and the horse while throwing occasional glances over to two other girls with blonde hair and indolent brown eyes, who had draped themselves over some chairs a short distance away and who looked as if they were waiting for something to happen, only it never did.

They were all dressed in much the same way, in European-style riding gear with their white jodhpurs and shiny black boots, tailored shirts and Gucci belts. They smoked extra-long cigarettes, played with gold lighters, and chatted and laughed with the kind of unselfconscious, sophisticated ease that a lot of money brings, as though it was growing on the trees around them while the sun shone and they didn't need to think about it.

There was no shortage of money in San Francisco Hacienda.

The whole place breathed money. The cars in the shadows were pricey, the big airy buildings were costly and the tiles on the floors were polished. The horses were polished. Even the young men and the girls were polished with their glossy hair and smooth skins, their rings and pearls and gold Cartier lighters.

Then one of the blonde girls called down to her friend with the horse in the manège to come and have a drink. She waved back, made the horse do another couple of circuits and signalled to the man with the big belly to stop him by the gate. He slipped a headcollar on to him and led him up towards the stables.

You could see the horse was glad to be out of the manège and going back to the stables.

He'd had enough of the manège.

The two young girls smiled and cooed as he walked past them and told their friend what a beautiful horse he was. A couple of the young men ambled over to pat him and make a fuss of him and told the man with the belly to hose him off and give him some lucerne.

The fat man looked at his feet, spat, and nodded.

He looked coarse and down-at-heel beside these elegant young men. And you could see he took what they said with a kind of peevish reluctance, which told you he knew what to do and resented being ordered around by blokes in posh clothes who made out they knew it all.

But he did what they said anyway and whistled a kind of a soft whistle to show he didn't care and hosed the horse off under the shade of the acacias, and the horse stretched his neck and pawed the ground and shook the water off in a brilliant momentary rainbow. Another fellow rubbed him dry and led him to a big clean stable where he turned to look back at what was happening to the other horses under the verandah, with the other grooms.

The young fellows who had been advising on how to hose him and what to do next, broke away and ambled through the verandah and hung over stable doors and advised the grooms on the best way to polish boots and clean tack. They patted the horses, pointing out good and bad features and all the time kept glancing back at the blonde girls, who talked and laughed and smoked and flicked cigarette ash over their shoulders. The other girl joined them and ordered freshly squeezed orange juice, which a waiter brought out to them on a small stainless-steel salver.

Then everything slowed to a long hot afternoon's languor. Cicadas rang in the trees, birds sang in the jacaranda, horses chewed in sleepy content, the grooms smoked and cleaned more boots. A breeze flickered the sun-dappled leaves on the gums and ice clinked in glasses.

Altogether, San Francisco is a calm and very classy place.

It's about six miles from Neza. And Neza is not a classy place.

Neza stinks.

It stinks because it lies in the lowest part of the old dried-up lakebed where the city's main sewage plant is; and it stinks because it's where every bit of garbage that gets slung out of Mexico City winds up.

To get there you drive past the prison, which sits in what looks like half-dried mud, and just behind the prison is the rest of the dump. At one time the dump spread right across the lakebed, right out past the prison, a couple of miles or more to the far side, but now a lot of it has been put down to grass. You could hardly tell from a distance it had not always been grass.

3

Still, it doesn't take long to see that what you are looking at is the lowest of the low and that this is rock bottom, the place where things wind up when they are completely finished with and have no value.

The sun was high and hot when we arrived and a man in a water bowser was blowing filthy water about on the dirt track to the dump, to damp down the dust. As we got out of the car the stench of the place slammed into us in a hot sickly wave that stank of sewage, sweating detritus and rotting carcasses.

On the edge of the dump nearest to us, a big-boned, broad-hipped Indian woman was sifting through the rubbish. She was very short, almost stubbily built, but colourfully dressed and you could hear her breathing. You could hear the noise of the rake she was using as she sorted out glass and cardboard, throwing them into small heaps beside her, and above this you could hear the erratic buzz of millions of flies.

There must have been about thirty people out on the dump altogether, sorting through the rubbish. They were out there with the ponies and donkeys they use to pull the *carretas* in which they collect the rubbish from town. And as they dragged the rubbish out of the *carretas*, the ponies and mules and donkeys just stood there in the stench and the flies, waiting for them to finish before hammering back down the hot streets into town to get another load.

We learned that they get the rubbish by driving round the streets with these *carretas* ringing a bell; then people come out and tip all their kitchen refuse into the *carretas* and part with a few pesos. They go on ringing their bells until the *carreta* is full, then turn round and whip the pony back to the dump, which could be anything up to five or six miles away. That's a long, hot slog in Mexico City with all its problems of pollution, lying as it does on an old lakebed surrounded by mountains, where the movement of air is slow and the traffic is dense.

When the horse and *carreta* reach the dump there's a short incline up to it and these little creatures have learned to pick up as much speed as they can in order to get up that incline. They strain on their harness and wind themselves up to hit the slope with all their might so as not to get bogged down on the edge, where they'd have to fight and be whipped to drag the thing into the middle.

You can see they've learned to do the slope trick all by themselves. They all do it: every one of those ponies or worn-out old horses, or sore-backed mules.

They do it because the *carretas* are awkward, heavy things.

They're a sort of metal-box arrangement bolted on to the axle of a scrap car, with the differential gearing still in place, so not only do the ponies have to draw the weight of the *carreta* and all the rubbish, but they have to turn the gearing as well. The whole thing must weigh something over a ton, which would feel more like two or three on that slope with the extra drag from the diffs.

So along the roads they come, moving as fast as they can, not only because they need to hit the dump at speed but because their feet are so sore that they can't put much weight on them for long and so it's easier for them to move quickly, even though they are sore and exhausted and their harness rubs.

The harness, such as it is, is crude, knocked-up stuff, most of it made of discarded and frayed nylon wrapped round plastic gunny bagging or corn sacking and knotted on the rib. What saddle-pads they have are sacking, too, thrown over a scrap of truck tyre, or anything that can be found in the rubbish. The saddle frame is saw-bench type, and takes the whole weight of the *carreta*, which is overcentred, and lies heavy on the animals' backs.

Mostly the animals were in poorish order and you could see they only just got enough to get by on, because there wasn't a centimetre of spare flesh on any of them.

And there they work, day in, day out, clattering down the road as fast as their legs can carry them with the drivers whacking them across their behinds and wrenching the bits in their mouths at the same time to get the most out of them.

They come in at a wild canter dragging this heavy *carreta* with the diffs spinning and as soon as they hit the dump, clouds of flies explode up in front of the ponies and settle all over them. Then the driver yanks on the reins and the pony stops, heaving and panting, and the men get off and prise the rubbish out, leaving the pony to grub about in the filth for a bite to eat, or something to sip on.

*

5

When we were there a sudden dust-devil hit the dump, whipping up a swirling vortex of plastic bags and rubbish and driving tiny sharp dirt particles into our eyes. It exposed all the composting underbelly of the tip and with it a stench rose, enough to make you vomit. But the little horses just blinked and shook their heads and the dust-devil swept over them, while the men kept on heaving out the rubbish. Then when they'd emptied the *carretas* they whipped the ponies up and took off back to town again.

Some drivers were meaner than others to their ponies but the worst I saw was a girl about seventeen years old. That little pony was so frightened of her, there was hardly a thing left of him. He was just black hide slung round a broken skeleton and she made him pull the biggest *carreta* there, all on his own, with his bad feet and sores under his breastplate.

And while I was watching her, a nearby *carreta* suddenly flipped up on its end and up went the shafts into the air, mule and all. That mule hung there completely exhausted until the men who had been unloading the *carreta* cut him free, and then he collapsed into the rubbish and they kicked him to his feet and harnessed him in again as soon as they'd righted the *carreta*.

In among all this the farriers worked: the ones that Walt trained.

Walt runs an organization called Working Together For Equines (WTFE). You won't find Walt in the posh end of town: you'll find him with his farriers down in the dump, in amongst the flies and the stink, working on the feet of the ponies and the mules which have just walked through that filth.

One walked straight through something which erupted when he trod on it and sprayed a jet of brown ooze up under his belly. The farrier shod him regardless, wiping the mess off and slapping a handful of citronella there, to sweeten it.

Walt just chuckled.

You need a sense of humour to cope with Neza.

*

The dump is run by a big woman who rents it from the lawyer who owns the land, and she's doing pretty well. She charges the people who use it 40,000 pesos a day, and on top of that she takes a cut on the litter they sort and a cut on what is sold. It's a system everyone understands, and they stick to it.

She was born and raised on dumps, and when we asked her what she'd do if the city council closed this one, she said she'd go right off and find another. Dumps were her life, she said, and the lives of the people who worked them. You couldn't change that, she said. These people knew no different and if everything else changed, they would stick with the dumps. They were poor by many standards, but they were better off than a lot of other people in the city. At least they had work and could make a bit on sorting tin and glass and clothes, plastic and cardboard. Sure, they could buy vans to do the work, but horses were a kind of tradition. Everyone who works on the dumps uses horses: everyone.

In the late afternoon we went to the kind of double-row shanty town on the edge of the dump where the people lived. They kept it pretty clean considering, and the first thing we saw was a group of girls washing clothes and pegging the clean washing out on lines. The girls were smiling, and the few children who hung around us were a knockout – pretty, grinning little children with big deep smiles and big brown eyes.

Behind where they were playing stood their shacks, and beside those, stable-blocks. Each horse lived according to his owner: some were kept in good little places, with roofs and bedding, and green feed, lucerne mostly. Others were kept any old how, in rough sheds with broken roofs, no bedding and not enough to eat.

Water was a problem. I saw no water for the horses except a single forty-gallon drum to which, when their owners remembered, they got taken for a drink.

Life's hard on Neza.

But Walt's farriers made it easier for the horses by trimming their feet and getting them fitted with good, even shoes. A well-shod horse can do more work than a poorly shod one, and by doing more work

7

he makes his owner more money. More money means a better life and a better life for his owner means more food for the pony.

Before Walt turned up the horses and mules and donkeys had to make do with rebar shoes, shoes made from metal reinforcing rods stolen from building sites and worked roughly into shape, then given a long uneven calkin for a heel. The farriers were untrained so the shoes went on roughly and the outcome was lame horses. But because life there is close to the bone, lame horses have to work.

Of all the horses down in Neza, there's one that sticks in my mind.

Even now I can see that old grey mare go trotting through the rubbish pulling that *carreta*. She was skin and bone: but she had dignity. Alongside her in the traces was a broken-down mule trying to keep up with her as she trotted along with her ears forward and head high, looking as dignified as she could; but the harness just rubbed the mule on one side because the mare was so much taller. He was having a bad time; and so was she.

You could see she had breeding, that mare. It's surprising the well-bred horses that wind up in Neza. Once she must have been a pretty nice horse, a real old favourite. Perhaps she'd been injured – from jumping or from careless handling, or just from bad luck – or perhaps she'd just grown old. Whatever the reason, when nobody wanted her any more she'd been sold for whatever she was worth, which wouldn't have been much, and so she wound up on Neza.

It could be that one day that big bay horse from San Francisco, the one with the metallic sheen on his coat – will end up in Neza, amongst the rubbish, pulling a *carreta*.

But if he does, maybe by then the farriers that Walt trained will be there to do his feet, and maybe André the saddler will be there to sort out his harness, to make life a little easier for him in his old age.

PART ONE

Cruelty in Context

Today the ILPH sends teams round the world to shoe horses and mules in places like Neza; to sort harness in Jordan, or India, or the Caribbean; to undertake veterinary work in Morocco or Israel; to manage horses in New Zealand or to oversee shipments of horses from South America to Europe. That it is able to operate on such an international scale – let alone all the work that has been done and still goes on in Britain – is a great tribute to the spirit that has imbued it since its earliest beginnings.

Its path has been long, and seldom easy. It has had to fight against vested interest, against ill-informed opinion, and at times against motives more sinister than either. For every fight won, there has always been another to take its place, and throughout its life the ILPH has constantly found itself having to steer a path through new and turbulent challenges.

But it has persisted, even when it stood alone. Most particularly when it stood alone, since when it began, the idea of animal welfare, although not new, was very far from being what it is today. Whatever its fortunes, it has continued to believe in its own philosophy: that its single and most important premiss is the welfare of the horse. It is not driven by sentiment, nor by a sanctimonious impulse to 'do good'. Nor has it ever set itself up as judge and jury to determine what a horse is supposed to do or not to do. Rather, it aims, by example, to correct, to train, and to educate; and by encouragement, to enable horses, ponies, donkeys and mules anywhere in the world to be given a fair chance to do a fair day's work under the best possible conditions. Where none of this is practicable, then it will step in, incisively, and rehabilitate any horse in distress.

Extracts from the ILPH *Annual Reports* 1966–72 express this philosophy succinctly and powerfully:

The policy of your Council is to abstain from accusations, all too often ill-founded, or worse, from sensational stories in the press, and quietly to investigate malpractices and complaints at first hand by our own accredited inspectors or representatives, and, where and when required, to act with determination and persistence to see wrongs righted or reforms set in motion till adopted and enforced. Let us be clear: where there is solid ground for it we are the last to muffle the voice of indignation, which we have raised to good purpose in the past, but let it be based on demonstrable facts, for these alone will validate the arguments to follow . . .

Let us again stress that where poverty and ignorance are the root of the trouble, where dire hardships of life make men harsh and even callous (for our experiences have shown that really malicious and cruel natures are uncommon), the finger-wagging and upbraiding critic will alter little and will be laughed to scorn when his back is turned . . . What lies in our power is to observe and instruct, to lend aid and not least, to set an example which by beneficial results will slowly attract followers and conduce to the welfare and relief of the animals we serve. In the long term it must be pressures from a more dissident people that will move mountains, and education and example are the best procedures where enlightened legislation is a nettle governments refuse to grasp. It is the native population that must be converted, for only their cumulative protests can force the issue.

The cruelty, neglect and ignorance which the ILPH strives to combat have, sadly, always been with us. But there is another, fundamental and quite different attitude which equally underpins the purpose of the ILPH and infuses every person who supports it: the special regard in which the horse has always been held by man; a regard which stems from a unique relationship of mutual dependence between man and animal.

I should like therefore in this chapter to look back over a broader, more retrospective canvas in order to examine briefly some of the attitudes, both of regard and of mistreatment, without which the ILPH would not have come into existence.

*

More than any other animal, perhaps, the horse is inextricably linked with human history. He has carried countless victorious armies, and has enabled whole nations to move on their migrations. His influence on our culture has been profound. For many people, the horse has been not just a workmate or a companion but a way of life. Nowhere is this impact better illustrated than on the plains of North America. There the horse was unknown to the Native Americans until it was introduced by the Spanish conquistadors in the sixteenth century; yet a mere 300 years later, life for the Sioux, the Cheyenne, the Kiowas and the other Plains tribes would have been unthinkable without the painted ponies which were their transport and their wealth, and on which they relied both for the hunt and for the warpath.

What distinguishes the special relationship between man and horse is that the horse is both companion and beast of burden, friend and workmate. He shares our lives and our affections in the same way as the animals we keep as pets. But we also work him and use his body for meat as we do other domestic livestock, cattle and sheep. On the one hand, man exploits the horse's usefulness, while on the other, he exalts his beauty, power and grace.

This has been true since the earliest times.

Current opinion is that the horse was first domesticated at least 4000 years ago on the steppes of Central Asia, by the Aryan tribesmen from whom are descended the Indo-European races, the Turkomans, the Persians, the warriors of Pakistan and Northern India, the Etruscans, the Scythians, the Norsemen and the Celts. To all these peoples, the horse has been in some sense or other a holy object.

The prehistoric Pazyryk horse burials of the Altai region of Siberia show the importance of the horse to its earliest domesticators: skeletons of stallions in ritual positions mark the graves of chieftains.

Certainly horses were vital to the Hittite empire in 1400 BC, and the same precept which inspires the ILPH today – the proper care of the horse – informs the earliest known written text on horses: the *Chariot Training Manual* of Kikkulis the Mittanite. The Parthian and Nisean horses of what is now Northern Iran were famed throughout the classical world and spread west into Europe as a result of Alexander the Great's conquest of the Persian Empire. The Celts were masters of horsemanship who used beautifully made jointed snaffle bits which, except for their carved and decorated rings, are exactly like the ones we use today. Yet with them they were able to control excited chariot ponies in the heat of battle, and their ability to negotiate difficult terrain and execute complicated manoeuvres at speed is commented upon by Julius Caesar in his account of his invasion of Britain in 54 BC. The Chinese in around 126 BC acquired a number of the 'heavenly horses' of Turkestan by exchanging them for an emperor's daughter, and again by laying siege to a town until the terms of surrender – a quota of horses – were met.

The various tribes who migrated from East to West – the Assyrians, Huns, Tartars, and the greatest of them all, the Mongols – literally lived on horseback. They ate and slept on their horses; they drank their horses' milk and sometimes their blood; they used their hides and their hair for the felt that made their tents and their saddles; they used their sinews to bind their bows and arrows.

These people, to whom the horse was, in every sense, their life, must have understood their horses and their care in a way that few people in our mechanical and industrialized world can do today.

There is no doubt that the horse occupied a special place in the minds of many of these ancient peoples. What inspired the Celts to carve the glorious, almost abstract representation of the White Horse on the Berkshire Downs? The white horse was a sacred symbol of the Saxons, too – hence the emblem of Kent – and in Vedic India they held the royal ritual of the *ashvamedha*, in which a white stallion was let loose to wander for a year, and the soldiers who followed it claimed all the land on which it trod in their ruler's name.

There is scarcely a part of the world in which the horse has not been accorded mythical status. The Greeks gave us Pegasus, the winged horse, and the centaur, in whom the body – the power – of the horse is united with the torso, arms and head – the dexterity and intellect – of man.

From biblical lands comes the story that Baz, great-great-grandson of Noah, was the first man to tame a wild horse. And since Mt Ararat, in the Caucasus, is not all that far from the Caspian Sea and the steppes of Turkmenistan, who knows – perhaps he was.

The Norse god Odin, the most shamanic of gods, had his horse Sleipnir, which represented both the wind and the mount on which the shaman rode to the spirit world.

In China, the Horse King, Ma-Wang, the Celestial Charger, was revered as the ancestor of all horses; and in Europe, the Gaulish horse goddess Epona was venerated by the Roman cavalry, who carried her worship throughout the Empire. Hinduism contends that when Vishnu appears for the tenth and last time at the end of this era it will be as Kalkin, a white horse.

And every hero had his horse. Rustum, the great Persian hero and subject of Matthew Arnold's poem *Sohrab and Rustum*, had his Raksh, of whom the Persian poet Firdausi says, 'his value was the whole of our Persian fatherlands'. In Ireland, Cuchulain, the Hound of Ulster, had his Grey of Macha, the *Liath Macha*, who, aware that his master was about to die in his final conflict with Queen Maeve of Connacht, refused to be harnessed to the chariot and wept tears of blood. Humbler horses and humbler heroes from more recent traditions are no less inseparable: who can think of Don Quixote without his Rosinante?

In history as in myth: immortalized in art and literature, sculpted in stone or bronze in a multitude of city squares, the names of horses resonate alongside those of the men who rode them. Alexander's Bucephalus; Richard II's Roan Barbary; Napoleon's Marengo; Wellington's Copenhagen; Traveller, who carried Robert E. Lee through the campaigns of Northern Virginia in the American Civil War. And from the steppes come tales of a nameless white stallion that haunts the grave of the greatest cavalry commander ever to sit astride a saddle: Genghis Khan.

From Central Asia to the field of Waterloo, these were hardheaded men who lived in a violent and often brutal world. What they felt for their horses was not sentiment, but fellowship, and it is this that is the constant theme that echoes down to us today. Ask any cavalryman the name of the horse he rode out from his barracks twenty, thirty years ago. Ask a jockey the name of his first winner, or a child the name of his first pony. Who ever forgets?

*

15

However, in the main, historically, those who had this special regard for the horse, the people who were steeped in every aspect of horsemanship, have tended to be the warrior aristocracy to whom the horse was both a military essential and a source of status. It was in their interest to maintain the best stock in the best condition possible, and the treatment of their horses reflected this. For the same reasons various English monarchs, from Athelstan in the tenth century to Henry VIII in the sixteenth, took measures to improve the native stock. Until the late medieval period, horses were rarely used as beasts of burden – oxen more usually fulfilling that lowly function – but were kept almost exclusively for pleasure or for war. They were the lucky ones.

The position today is very different. In many of those countries whose ancient peoples venerated the horse he is now no more than an economic unit, and the bottom line, the lowest economic denominator, is what dictates the quality of his care. And it is in some of these countries – the Middle East and Eastern Europe – that the work of the ILPH is needed most.

The treatment of horses has reflected, too, the attitude of the ordinary man in the street towards animals in general, and this has varied considerably in different cultures and in different eras. There have always been those who have advocated kindness. Plutarch wrote pamphlets on the protection and better husbandry of animals and maintained that much could be learned from them, since they behaved with natural dignity and with greater moral correctness than man. The philosopher Porphyry spoke out for the protection of livestock generally, but for any horseman, all other classical authors are over-shadowed by Xenophon, the Greek scholar and general whose book, the *Treatise on Horsemanship*, is as bright and enjoyable as any book on horses to come off the printer's block today, and just as instructive as most.

Xenophon implored his cavalry to look to their horses' well-being, and especially to take care of their feet, because as he himself first told us, 'where there is no hoof there is no horse'. Without four good feet, a horse is useless. Moreover, he cautioned his cavalrymen that the gentle hand was better than the rough, and would be the hand the horse would trust in the face of attack; and because of that trust the horse would be less likely to turn and bolt, trampling his own ranks behind him.

Xenophon argued that between a horseman of understanding and his mount a spiritual relationship develops. This is not sentiment, but an acknowledgement of the degree of communication that can be achieved between man and horse, as when the rider's aids are given so imperceptibly, and the horse responds so immediately, that the partnership seems almost intuitive. In the days when a man's life could depend on his horse, such understanding was a practical necessity, and you can see it today in the disciplines of dressage and *haute école*, or on the ranches of America and Australia where cattle horses interpret their riders' wishes to cut out stock.

Most riders, even the most sceptical, will prefer to get to know one individual horse rather than many, to ride him and learn his ways and paces and idiosyncrasies, just as that horse will learn the characteristics of his rider, and the relationship that develops will be as deep or as shallow as the rider himself. The nineteenth-century writer R. S. Surtees echoed Xenophon's point with his famous comment that 'there is no secret so close as that between a rider and his horse'.

Many of the world's religions have preached kindness to animals. It was a powerful force in Zoroastrianism, as it is in Islam and in Buddhism, and of course Jain monks will harm no creatures at all, sweeping insects out of their path as they travel on their way.

Omar, general of the Prophet Mohammed, exhorted his troops to 'love horses, tend them well for they are worthy of your tenderness: treat them as members of the family, feed them like children, clothe them with care. For the love of Allah do not neglect to do this or you will repent for it in this house and the next.' The Prophet himself promised the indulgence of Allah to any sinner who gave a grain of barley to a horse.

The Old Testament has allusions to helping others with their animals in distress, and in Deuteronomy 22:4 it reads: 'Thou shalt not see thy brother's ass or his ox fall down by the way and hide thyself from them: thou shalt surely help him to lift them up again.'

Christianity itself had no specific injunction to act kindly towards animals. As far as the church was concerned animals had no souls and it was therefore no crime to treat them as chattels, to be used and thrown away. Nowadays, happily most Christians would apply

17

Christian principles to animals as well as to people and would argue that it is no more permissible to be cruel to them than to fellow humans.

St Francis of Assisi is acknowledged as the patron saint of animals, and it is said that he once visited Jeladdin Al Rumi, the great Sufi master, who shared his sense of compassion for all living things. But horses have their own saint in the mysterious St Hippolytus, to whom the church of St Ippollitts just outside Hitchin in Hertfordshire is dedicated. Horses have been blessed here for centuries – some say that the Crusaders brought their horses here on their way to the Holy Land – and even recently services have been held to commemorate this tradition.

Those who lived and worked with horses in medieval Europe were no less mindful of the importance of proper care and management than we are today. Medieval chronicles attested to 'the virtues of a good waggoner' as being 'those of modest expediency, not wrathful, but skilfully directing his horses and not overloading them'. A Tudor bestseller, Thomas Tusser's *Five Hundred Points of Good Husbandry* is a mine of information, its advice still as pertinent as it was when it was written, over four hundred years ago. In it he insists 'that good provender labouring horses would have, good haie and good plenty . . .' and instructs the horsekeeper:

> Look well to thy horses in stable thou must,
> that haie be not foistie, nor chaffe ful of dust:
> Nor stone in their provender, feather, nor clots,
> Nor fed with green peason, for breeding of bots.

Who would have read these early books on husbandry? It was pretty unlikely to have been the waggoners themselves, who were probably no more literate than the horses they drove. Perhaps they were read by the more educated, go-ahead yeomen farmers. I can imagine his trying to put his knowledge into practice, chiding some rugged old waggoner for thrashing his worn-out horse, pleading with him to do it another way, a gentler way, and being told, in not so many words, to take his 'pleading' ideas elsewhere.

Habits die hard. It happens today. Nobody likes to be told how to handle his horse. Nobody.

Yet thoughtless treatment of draught animals is a story the world over, and everywhere, England included, a horse's hesitancy is often taken for stupidity and the cautious and frightened animal, lost for a moment's comprehension, is punished as a result.

How often do you hear of a rider making the effort to understand the language of his horse?

England, 'the nation of animal lovers', was itself at one time known as 'the hell of horses'.

No one who has read Anna Sewell's *Black Beauty* can forget her descriptions of overworked, beaten and broken-kneed cab horses and draught horses on the streets of Victorian cities. Rightly recognized as a children's classic, *Black Beauty* was nevertheless written with a serious purpose, as a protest against the plight of the horses whose suffering its author witnessed. Fashion, as ever, played its part in cruelty here: Anna Sewell painted a vivid picture of horses struggling against overtight bearing reins, their heads strapped artificially high, unable to use their proper strength to pull their loads as a result.

The best part of a hundred years before *Black Beauty* was written, Jeremy Bentham, the moral philosopher, spoke out against the whipping of horses on the streets of London, as did Hogarth, Cowper and Blake. Lord Erskine was reputed to have stopped a man beating his horse on Hampstead Heath, whereupon the irate horseman turned to the Lord Chancellor and retorted that he could do what he liked with what he owned. The noble lord answered him with a volley from his own cane, saying that the same law therefore applied to him, since he owned his cane.

William Wilberforce – he of the anti-slavery laws – joined his voice to the outcry for animal welfare, and from this groundswell of opinion, in 1826, sprang the origins of the society which was later to become the RSPCA. Its founding spirit was a man called Richard Martin, gentleman, who had 200,000 acres in Ireland and was known as Humanity Dick, or the Wilberforce of animals, in recognition of his work. From him resulted a whole string of acts of Parliament designed to improve the treatment of animals in England, among them attempts to end cock-fighting and bull-baiting, and to ameliorate, a little, the terrible conditions in slaughterhouses.

*

That society whose roots began in 1826 had on its Council, a century later, a woman called Ada Cole. At the age of fifty-one, Ada Cole was provoked into action by a sight that motivated her for the rest of her life and impelled her to take up the battle against cruelty and indifference on behalf of horses. Her Old Horse Traffic Committee – in some sense a foster-child of the RSPCA, though the relationship was never other than a stormy one – later became the International League Against the Export of Horses for Butchery, and in 1937 became the International League for the Protection of Horses – the name we know today.

The work she began on flimsy finances when she saw English horses bound for slaughter on the docks of Antwerp has developed into the world's largest privately endowed equine charity, which has set itself a charter to do exactly what its title conveys: protect horses.

Its task has been a hard one. Many of its activities are still connected with working or draught animals, since by far the majority of horses, mules and donkeys work as beasts of burden in poorer countries, and their lot in life is usually a miserable one. But – and this point is central to the work of the ILPH abroad – if any improvement is to be made in the way people in poor countries treat their horses, it will be because those people have been brought to see that such improvement is in their own economic interests. The absence of money makes life hard, and what affects an animal's existence in these countries most of all is ready cash, or the lack of it: in general, the poorer the country, the more brutal the treatment of animals appears to be. Only governments can make wholesale changes in economies: but every human being can be motivated by the chance to make something of himself, to stand on his own two feet. This is why education plays such a large part in the campaigns of the ILPH: show a man how to shoe his horse so that it will not fall lame, how to harness his donkey so that it can go on working more easily, and you give him the chance to improve his own lot; train a lad in Mexico to be a farrier to his mates' horses and you offer him in exchange for a perhaps hopeless life the chance of a half-decent one.

There are, of course, cases – and countries – where ill-treatment of horses seems to come not from the indifference of grinding poverty but from a brash machismo expressed in terms of an idiotic brutality. If you look closely at such behaviour, you will see hidden within it that most pernicious form of cruelty – to hurt the animal before it hurts you. Such treatment stems not from masculine pride, nor from tradition – my grandfather did it this way, and so shall I – but from simple fear of a loss of control. Thus, even apparently mindless cruelty can in fact spring from an attitude of mind, and attitudes can, with the right approach, be changed. This is the ultimate goal which the ILPH sets itself in its work around the world.

Remote as many Third World countries might seem to us, their position on the world stage unlit, there are other countries nearer home, in the ex-Communist bloc of Eastern Europe, where some of the sights and sounds are not so far removed from those of North Africa or Latin America.

In the backstreets of Ihtiman in Bulgaria or on the high street of Samokov, you'll find horses working in the heat of summer and the snows of winter, slapping round the streets pulling wooden carts. And if the horse is a mare the chances are she'll have a foal with her and the foal will be running alongside her tied with a piece of string. Their owner will be sitting on the cart, wrapped up against the slicing Balkan winds, and he'll be weaving the mare and her foal down cobbled alleys through the town, collecting rubbish.

If you go to Romania, to Almuşu Mare or to Coren, you'll find horses looking very much the same, pulling carts, only these horses will be used for farm work, and if they are state-owned horses, they'll be in poor condition.

On up through Hungary you'll see more draught horses – not big heavy horses like ours, but lighter creatures, and usually dark bay or black. You'll find the same in Slovakia and Poland and what was East Germany. You'll find them all the way across the Ukraine and right across Russia as far as Yakutia and beyond, from the Caucasus and South Central Asia, from Khiva down the Oxus to Samarkand, and the greater part of these will be working horses.

As foals they will have trotted alongside their mother round the villages, or they might have accompanied her as she pulled the drays of commerce, or lugged farm waggons, or harvested the fields of the collectives. When he grew older the foal would have been allowed to run free beside the mare until the day came to break him to harness. Then, in the words of the ILPH Eire *Annual Report* of 1962:

> ... from the moment the colt is first put under the plough or between the shafts the sentence is hard labour for life. No remission for good conduct, in his case; no hope of freedom when that sentence expires, and no peace, or well-deserved rest in the fields he has sown and reaped all his life. Far from it: his owner decides that he must earn money by dying as well as living, and the sentence of hard labour is changed to exportation and capital punishment.

The horses of Eastern Europe and Russia suffer today the same fate as the workhorses of Britain when the ILPH began. After a lifetime's work they are exported hundreds, sometimes thousands of miles overland by truck or train for slaughter, with nothing to eat throughout the journey and often no water. This, to those of finer sensibilities, is a bitter betrayal of an animal that has given his life to the service of man.

No other animal has so decisively been the companion of man, none has shared his life as closely nor offered such abundant versatility: he is ploughman, harvester, drawer of chattels and the munitions of war; he is policeman, armour bearer, entertainer, sportsman, water carrier, grinder of corn, clown – and he has been used to transport his own kind to slaughter.

Is it so much to ask that we return to his descendants a grain of the debt we owe him?

It is not the slaughter of the horse at the end of his working life that is at issue here. It is the thoughtless way in which he is transported to that slaughter and the often needlessly barbaric circumstances in which that slaughter is carried out.

And it was precisely these concerns which motivated Ada Cole to set out and redress those wrongs over sixty years ago. Since then many Acts and Orders over half a century have ensured the better treatment of horses, ponies, mules and donkeys the world over. She might well have been surprised to know that there followed in her footsteps men and women of real resolve, moved, like her, not by sentimental appeal but by a sense of right and decency and the acknowledgement of a moral obligation.

Through them, the officers and members who give their support, their time and their donations to its activities, millions of horses have felt the hand of the ILPH upon them.

PART TWO

Women and Horses and Power and War: The Early Days of the ILPH

ONE

A da Cole was born in 1860, six years after 700 British horsemen charged a battery of Russian guns at the head of a Balaclava valley in the Crimea.

She was born into a family of gentlemen farmers, daughter of Noah Edward Cole and his wife Louisa of Croxton Hall Farm, Croxton, just outside Thetford, Norfolk. Her upbringing, if not privileged, was certainly comfortable.

I am told that she was the seventh child of a seventh child, although in the parish register, now kept in the main library in Norwich, she appears as the fourth child. But families were large in the Victorian era and it is quite possible that stillborn births might have been counted into family numbers. So she might well have been the seventh of the seventh and imbued therefore with all the mystique that that event signifies.

Her father farmed 1100 acres, employing between eighteen and twenty men on the farm and in the census of 1870, when she would have been ten, she is described, along with her sister, as a 'scholar'.

In her twenties she became a nurse, and in 1886, the year before Queen Victoria's Golden Jubilee, she moved to London, where her sister Effie had joined the Little Sisters of the Assumption. Although Ada lived with the nuns for a while, she did not become a novice. Effie went on to become a Reverend Mother, and moved from London to Ireland and thence to Belgium, where Ada followed her.

In 1900 she went back to Norfolk and became a district nurse in Norwich – the town where Anna Sewell had written *Black Beauty*. During this time she was a frequent visitor to markets in King's Lynn, where cattle and horses were abominably treated, and she made her views known. It was already clear that hers was a spirit alien to compromise, although the real tests of its power and strength were still to come.

In 1910, the year King Edward VII died, she bought Hill Top

in Cley-next-the-Sea. This small rose-covered cottage was set high above the marsh, about half a mile's walk from the windswept shore at Cley, where she was to spend so much time later on, pacing the long shaly beach as she formulated speeches and worked out tactics for the campaigns which finally drove her into the public eye.

I visited Cley with Kay Watson from the ILPH, who sought out and found a remarkably bright old lady whose mother used to keep the post office. Miss Starr was ninety-three when Kay and I talked to her but her memory was as clear as Cley is pretty, and she recalled Ada Cole coming into the post office dressed as a district nurse.

An article we unearthed in the *Eastern Daily Press*, written by a man going duck flighting with a couple of locals, offered us another glimpse. On their way to the sea bank they passed a diminutive figure wrapped in a dark cloak, who made no reply 'when Bob called out "Good night, Miss Cole!" Perhaps she did not hear – and perhaps she did, for Bob stopped for a moment, and as the lady passed on murmured, "That's Miss Cole who lives on Hill Top – all Miss Cole thinks about is animals." Deeply have I regretted that I did not make her acquaintance in those far off days,' he writes, 'when I might have called upon a woman in whose fragile frame flamed the courage and indignation worthy of that of Nurse Cavell.'

It was in the spring of 1911, while visiting her sister Effie in Belgium, that Ada was apprehended by a sight which was to alter completely the course of her life.

On the docks in Antwerp were horses, old horses, worn-out, galled, exhausted workhorses: lines of them, roped roughly together three abreast, being whipped along a four-mile stretch of road to slaughter. It was a ghastly procession. The horses were mere skeletons; with skin dry as parchment and sunken eyes, they hobbled before the whips on sore and ageing pasterns.

These were English horses. For the greater part they were heavies, but among them were vanners and cobs, carriage horses and hunters. Those that could not walk were hauled, heaved or beaten into creaking floats, pulled by their stumbling fellows, to their brutal end. Many lay still where they had fallen. In the Place de la Duchesse others stood heads bowed, or collapsed on the cobbles, waiting for buyers to pay the pittance to slave the last inch out of them on Belgian soil.

The trade was not illegal, and there were a great many culls to be had, geldings (traditionally) from towns and mares (usually) from farms. Their numbers on the docks were increasing as the rise in urban mechanization put more and more horses out of work.

Although some people still clung to the belief that horse power was superior to mechanical power, the problem was not that straight-forward. Until the turn of the century, many road surfaces had been made of granite stone setts, so that horses shod in the Liverpool style with calkins at the heel and a grip on the toe could get some purchase on their footing. With the advent of motorized power, road surfaces changed to tarmac, and the result was slick surfaces and sliding horses. One Cotswold farmer was reputed to have advertised for horses that could skate!

As mechanical vehicles became more common, London streets became intolerably jammed, and horses suffered: they were con-tinually slipping and traffic was constantly being held up as a result. Matters came to a head in 1924 when a two-hour jam on Blackfriars Bridge led to the London and Home Counties Traffic Advisory Committee proposing that the number of horses on the streets should be limited.

Not everyone agreed. Breed societies in particular had a strong interest in defending the superiority of the draught horse over the combustion engine, and by way of proving their case staged a weight-pulling contest at Wembley in 1924 between two Shires and a truck in which the Shire pair pulled a fifty-ton deadweight from a standstill, a feat which could not be equalled by the lorry. On farms, early tractors were clumsy, unmanoeuvrable things which frequently became mud-bound, and which could not travel along roads because of their iron spade wheels.

Horse power was not only more efficient, but more economic. A draught horse cost approximately one-tenth of its mechanical counterpart and had a working life of over fifteen years as opposed to five. Jobs depended on them: draymen, removal men, chandlers, harness makers, ostlers – of which there were thousands.

Eventually, however, the battle was lost.

Between 1909 and 1911, all horse-drawn trams had been withdrawn by the London Omnibus Company. And as Henry Ford's cheap Model Ts and other inexpensive vehicles came on to the market, so the value of horses at home fell. They became instead a source of ready export capital.

Ada Cole was a farmer's daughter and was no doubt aware of the economic arguments. But what she saw on the docks at Antwerp was an indictment of the market forces which dictate that where profit rules, the first casualty is always compassion: living animals become no more than a bulky commodity.

Although the trade was not illegal, it was conducted under a cloak. Dealers were anxious to keep their activities quiet and few people wanted to know in detail what happened to their old horses once they had fetched what they could get.

Nevertheless, it was a trade which revolted most decent people. Even the Belgians themselves who lived near the docks drew their curtains on the days the awful procession passed their windows.

But Ada Cole never shrank from witnessing appalling spectacles. She had no patience for the person who cried out 'Oh please don't tell me, I can't bear to hear' when some abuse of animals was being described. 'It is your duty to hear,' she would point out angrily. 'It is because people do not want to hear that nothing is done. I am going to make people listen.'

From that moment her life's pattern was set: she was to champion the cause of old horses.

She was joined by Jules Rhul, President of the Brussels Society for the Protection of Animals, who, like her, did not shrink from the work, and like her, was not intimidated by dealers who wanted no part of their sordid trade revealed to a larger world.

Rhul, she wrote, 'joined hands with me, and together we followed the horses, day and night, from landing to death. Week after week and month after month we saw the same terrible suffering.'

On another occasion she wrote: 'I met the horses in Antwerp and walked with them. There were two trolleys, a horse in each. They were still breathing. But they were dying and had been sent from England in that state after a life of ungrudging toil.'

Her work took her to even more dreadful places, the worst of which was the slaughterhouse of Vaugirard, in Paris.

Ada Cole never left us with an accurate description of Vaugirard but Patrick Keatley, special correspondent for the *Manchester Guardian*, left us with an unforgettable image:

> The huge slaughterhouse at Vaugirard stands in a depressing suburb in the south-west part of Paris. I arrived there in mid-morning to be greeted by an enormous metal sign high on the fortress-like walls which proclaimed: 'Les Abattoirs Hippophagiques. L'Entrée de L'Abattoir est Rigoureusement Interdite au Public' . . . the place is a vast sweep of cobbles and concrete in the middle of which are grouped the stables and slaughterhouses proper. The area, which is the size of a dozen soccer fields, is protected by stone walls and iron spikes; a bastion affair at one corner accommodates a Prefecture de Police, and another police station is set up near the actual slaughter floor with windows looking in two directions . . . The horses were led in from trucks, passing the following sequence of scenes as I saw them: a loading platform stacked with neatly folded moist hides, steaming in the sunshine; fresh hides just peeled from their owners with fat and blood still clinging and the face and snout formations still recognisable – these just six feet away from where the horses had to walk; and a large open area where a bay gelding was shuddering in its last agonies, a rush of crimson welling from its throat and its forelegs twitching in spasms.

Another witness wrote:

> I arrived outside Vaugirard market at 11.30. Both gates were guarded by policemen, so I did not attempt to enter but watched the market through open railings. I roughly estimated there to be between three and four hundred horses in the market. Many horses were in such appalling condition that they were mere skeletons. Others, in fair condition were suffering from extreme exhaustion. The general types were light vanners, heavy draughts, well-bred hacks, hunters and ponies. When I reached the main gate of the abattoir there were several men about – no police. Watching my opportunity I slipped in at the main gate at the far end of the yard.

There were horses there; they had practically no bedding, no feed. They were starving ... Butchers were busy cutting up carcases, blood and entrails were everywhere and in full view of the killing were the horses tethered.

I do not take pleasure in the bloodiness of this writing, and thought to omit it. But if I did, I should be guilty of the very thing Ada Cole condemned. The descriptions here are the descriptions given to the British public.

The killing was done by hammer, and sometimes pole-axe.

A six-pound mallet was slammed into the horse's skull, which sometimes, but not always, brought the horse to its knees. Often there were glancing blows when the slaughtermen missed, where eye sockets and nasal bones were shattered as the horse threw its head up (and most horses will throw their heads up when threatened from the front). Then mayhem followed as the terrified horse hurled itself about as the slaughterman rained blows on it until it fell again and then, if the second or third time the animal struggled to its feet, a knife was plunged into its chest and its jugular slashed open.

There it was left to thrash itself to death.

There was a reason behind this slow and painful end. The longer the horse takes to die, the whiter the meat.

Even more horrific was a device known as a blood pump, which was attached to the horse's neck and literally plumbed into its jugular. This device siphoned the blood out of the living horse, which fell and thrashed – an action which was encouraged because it had the effect of purging blood from the muscle.

The white meat could then be offered for sale as veal.

Some horses were sold for vivisection to the veterinary colleges. Ada Cole had proof that no anaesthetic was used and that horses were dismembered fully conscious, although restrained in order to prevent them injuring the students who were performing their morbid and Frankensteinian autopsies upon their living subjects.

All of this was happening against the backcloth of Europe approaching war. Yet the efforts Ada put into drawing public attention to the plight of horses was having effect, and resulted in an Act of Parliament in 1914 which amended previous laws. Up until then, the main law affecting the traffic in horses was a Government Order issued in 1898. This order prohibited the transit from any port in Great Britain of any horse which, owing to age, illness, injury, fatigue or any other cause, could not be conveyed without cruelty during the intended voyage and on landing. But this proved to be a non-starter. The regulations looked well enough on paper, but in practice their application was left to the discretion of local authorities, which more often than not meant that they were not applied at all. And who was to say what constituted cruelty, since there was no specific legal definition of the term.

In 1909 an Inspector of the Ministry of Agriculture was appointed to supervise the shipment of horses at various points. The traffic in slaughter horses had by this time increased to a lively business and in order to regulate it, the Diseases of Animals Act was brought in the following year. This prohibited the shipment of horses unless certified by a veterinary inspector 'to be capable of being conveyed and disembarked without cruelty', and also required every vessel carrying horses to be provided with a proper humane killer.

A further Act was forced through the Commons in 1914, which amended the previous measures by stating that a horse could not be exported unless it was 'capable of being worked as well as conveyed without suffering'.

Nevertheless, suffering and ill-treatment continued until on 28 June 1914, the export trade in horses came to an abrupt end when Gavrilo Princip in Sarajevo fired the shot that plunged Europe into war.

TWO

When the Great War broke out, Ada Cole was in Belgium staying with her sister in a convent. Since the war had ended the trade in the export of live horses – with the exception of horses required by the army – she returned to her former job as a nurse.

But she was a woman of causes and before long she had found another. Along with her sister Effie she worked among both the Allied and German wounded, and became involved in activities which eventually aroused the suspicion of the German military authorities. She wrote:

> For a long time after the German occupation, we helped men to cross the frontier in a haphazard fashion. We gave them money if they wanted it, and the address of a guide, or friends at a frontier town or village. We knew such helping was an offence, and punishable. But we had a vague idea it was not very grave. We did not know the Germans then, or their spies.
>
> In the same light-hearted way we hid wounded soldiers, got them false passports, and smuggled them into Holland. A group of sympathetic neighbours came to see two off from my sister's convent. A tramwayman, who she had helped over, sent his thanks, and his photograph in khaki, in a smuggled letter.
>
> When an Antwerp Jesuit was sentenced to fifteen years' hard labour, and, at about the same time, Miss Cavell was shot, we understood the risk.
>
> I have heard Miss Cavell and the men she helped blamed for indiscretion. Only people who were not in Belgium then, or who did nothing, and knew nothing of patriotic work could blame so unjustly. No one could realise the danger before penalties were inflicted or known ... The Jesuit who was sentenced to fifteen years' hard labour was convicted of the same offence as Miss Cavell, collecting young men and sending them over the frontier. It was not

34

spying, and ought not to have been punished with death. The shooting of Miss Cavell was an act of deliberate malignity against the English and whoever tries to throw the blame on her, or those she helped is speaking in defence of the Germans.

Patriots work and die. Those who do nothing, live; and criticise.

After Miss Cavell was shot people were careful.

Despite being 'careful', both Ada and Effie were arrested for complicity and imprisoned in the Antwerp Military Prison, of which she wrote:

The first phase of prison for those who are required to answer questions is 'secret'. An iron door bangs into an iron-bound doorway, a key grates in a lock, and the prisoner stands in his cell. The floor is flagged, the walls are drab yellow. There is a small treble-barred window high in the thick wall. There is a folding bed-table; a small jug of water in a basin on a shelf; an iron pail with a cover, in a cupboard under a shelf and a dustpan and brush. On another small cupboard with a shelf in it are two basins, and a spoon. In the folding bed are a dirty mattress, pillow and blanket. On the floor under it is a small piece of wood. So small a bit of sky can be seen through the window that prisoners cannot tell whether it is fine weather or it is raining. Three times a day food is brought ... pencils are taken away. The prisoner never leaves his cell for an instant, except to go down and be questioned by the police ... 'Secret' is meant to break down the courage or nerves of a prisoner so that he may give information. It generally lasts for weeks, till the police find out what they want to know ... The one duty of the prisoner is to baulk the police. Often he must either lie, or betray. Often he must give the lie direct to a traitor who is telling the truth. The general rule was to deny everything.

When a prisoner declares he is innocent the police can't question him without accomplices. They use bribes, threats, and traps to get the information they want. They promise freedom at once for betrayal. They threaten to arrest relatives or friends, or deportation to Germany. If a prisoner is too obstinate, or shows temper, they can order 'cachot' – that is, dungeon: semi-darkness, plank bed and bread and water.

It is difficult to occupy oneself in 'secret'. There are writings scratched on the walls, some brave, some terrible, some impudent, and partly erased. There are also long lists of dates with day after day scratched off. There is no other way of keeping count of time. As the light passed along the wall we could sometimes just make out another word ... we tapped the walls and our neighbours tapped back. That gave a feeling of comradeship.

And later:

Two prison vans took us to our trial.

Black Maria is not bad if you have the space and air holes meant for one person. Three of us were crammed into that space, and the broad back of a German soldier was against the door that shut us in.

The trial was a solemn farce.

It is pretty certain that the verdict and sentence are settled beforehand, on the evidence obtained by the Secret Police.

Immediately before the trial prisoners are allowed free communication with each other. But the row of officers took oaths solemnly, with uplifted hand, heard what we had to say and sentenced us.

So we were jolted back to prison again in our dark carriage. We, and the others sang patriotic songs and thumped an accompaniment. It cheers up passers-by to hear songs coming from the prison van. Whether or not punishment follows, depends on the guard.

Three months and fifteen days after our arrest came the Armistice and freedom. And my chief recollection of prison is of a splendid lot of women, always on the look-out to help each other and to defy the enemy. They were brave, clever and gay. One of the merriest was under sentence of death.

Ada too was under sentence of death. Even so, such was her lack of concern for herself that while in prison she complained to the prison Commandant about the state of pigs in an adjoining compound. The piggeries were cleaned up and the pigs fared better – which no doubt did little to commute Ada's sentence or improve her own circumstances.

Spared the firing squad by a timely Armistice, after the war she was honoured by King Leopold of Belgium and awarded the Décoration Civique for her part in securing the escape of patriots.

In January 1919, at the age of fifty-eight, she left Belgium, returned to nursing in Norwich and settled in Cley.

No sooner had she resumed her busy though relatively quiet life than she came across shipments of horses at King's Lynn, and discovered to her fury that not only was the 1914 Act unenforced but that it had failed even to be enacted owing to the ban on all horse exports at the outbreak of war.

At once she returned to the ships and their cargoes of heavy horses, vanners, cobs, weak and emaciated hunters bound for the pole-axes of Vaugirard. Once more, she became the self-appointed scrutineer, much to the anger of the dealers and slaughtermen she confronted.

It was not the human consumption of horsemeat that offended her, but that animals should be subjected to such indifferent and thoughtless treatment at the end of their lives. Constantly she advocated the establishment of a trade in dressed carcasses in preference to live animals, arguing that not only was it more humane, but that in a land where the heroes of war found themselves jobless, work would be generated through the by-products of the trade: what the Italians call the fifth quarter, the hoof, the hair and the hide.

What she sought above all was an Act of Parliament which would finally put a stop to the traffic of live horses for slaughter. For this she fought, and fought hard. She knew well there was little point in standing on the dockside, on ships or in slaughterhouses complaining. She went to these places to gather information at her own expense; by no means rich, she had some personal funds, and living frugally, used these to good purpose. Having got her evidence, what she needed was political clout, political capital, political allies.

To publicize her aims she toured the country, concentrating on Manchester and Birmingham, from which cities she received her strongest support. The *Manchester Guardian* became an important ally, publishing her reports and thereby gaining the attention of Members of Parliament and other men and women of influence.

Although not in good health – she was a phthisis sufferer – she made little of either the physical or mental pressures of her campaigning. Having seen what she had seen, having been interrogated, insulted, humiliated and put through all the devices of a modern inquisition in her prison camp in Belgium, she was equal to any challenge. Impossible to intimidate, she countered every argument thrown at her with demonstrable fact. This determination and resilience was what drew a core of influential friends to her cause.

The backcloth of the times revealed a changing scene. George V was on the throne, Lloyd George was Prime Minister and the suffragette movement had secured the vote for women. These were the Roaring Twenties. For some, it was boom time. The war was over and gone, and the young danced their nights away to the Charleston. London was a playground for the rich, and these were carefree days for them: times to forget the past, enjoy the present and not worry about the future. Cars were rolling off production lines and tractors out of factories. The great mechanical drive was on. But there was a great division in society. The larger part of it was looking into empty cupboards and at empty plates.

For the poor, it was desperate. Ramsay MacDonald formed his first Labour Government in 1924. But it didn't last long. By October it was all over and Stanley Baldwin took his chair. The economy was paying the price of war. What work there was was badly paid and the country headed inexorably toward the General Strike of 1926 and Depression.

All over the country, horses were being replaced by machines, and the price paid for them reflected it.

In her pursuit of funds and prominent supporters, Ada Cole appealed to the RSPCA. But money and official backing were slow in coming. Her frustration at this is evident in this extract from the first *Annual Report* of the International League Against the Export of Horses for Butchery:

> In 1922 at the invitation of the Council I took this special work into the RSPCA hoping to gain the help of its immense finance and organization against the traffic (in live horses for export). I will only say here that these hopes were not realised: that, for the sake of the horses, I had to oppose the Council and appeal against its members; and that members of that society helped me to form a Committee to carry on the work, and requisitioned an Extraordinary Meeting of the Society to deal with the situation. At the meeting a resolution

was passed by a great majority, calling on the Council to set up a department to carry on vigorously a campaign against the traffic, and to make me Organiser of that work. That meeting, the Council has to this day ignored. It was not even mentioned in their annual report.

And she goes on: 'The attitude of the Council towards the export of horses for butchery, and my appeal to the members, was the origin of a sharp division between Council and members.'

Finally, on 15 January 1925, she was appointed a permanent member of the RSPCA staff with a specific brief to research the horse traffic. She said she had already enough research material to make this unnecessary and had plenty of evidence to support her claims. Had she not given them details of conditions at Vaugirard? But she was told that because it had not been gathered in an official capacity none of her evidence would be considered, and that any evidence presented must be collated with an official delegation who had given prior notice to the slaughterhouse of their desire to inspect.

This, she said, was useless. Any warning of a visit resulted in a lightning clean-up and by the time the officials came, everything would be in order. What needed to be hidden was hidden.

So in February of that year she produced a pamphlet in which a Mr G. Harrison, an Englishman living in Paris, reported:

... on 16 September 1924 I saw at Vaugirard the employees of a horse dealer who buys very largely from Great Britain, use the following methods of dragging an injured horse from the stables to the dealer's slaughter shed.

The horse in question being unable to stand, its legs were roped to prevent it kicking, and another rope was tied from it to the tail of a second horse, which was then urged to drag the injured animal bodily from the stables across the cobbled yard and onto the floor of the shed, bumping down a pavement in course of route. As the towing horse was restive, both from the stench from the slaughter shed, and probably also from some degree of pain at this strange method of harnessing, the journey was made by a series of jerks, accompanied by moans from the injured animal. About six men assisted in this operation, their assistance consisting of shouts and laughter. It lasted, while I was there, for six minutes, but the operations had already started when I came upon the scene. Once in the slaughter shed the injured animal lay upon the blood-covered floor for a further three or four minutes before being despatched. The horse which had been used for towing was then returned to the stables to await its turn; this horse was one of a consignment which had arrived from England the previous day. I was told that this method was used because the trolley, used in such cases, was broken. Later, and by another informant, I was told that the trolley was not broken, but was at hand, and the men had not troubled to fetch it ... I have myself on several occasions seen a horse struck twice with the hammer before falling; on one occasion I saw one fall at the second blow but still live. It seemed to be about to rise, but a man held its head, a blood pan was slid under, and ...

Another piece of evidence, given later, spoke of 'one man, who through sheer devilment, took a handful of blood out of the pan and poured it into the beast's eyes whilst they were still rolling about in their death agony'.

These pamphlets were seen by the RSPCA as a potential cause of trouble. Discussion about them was often lengthy and heated, until finally it was agreed that they could be issued provided they were accompanied by the signature of the Chief Secretary.

This Ada Cole ignored. What the country needed to know was the truth about where their horses were going and what happened to them when they got there. People began to listen.

But then came scandal. A report of the Departmental Committee of the Ministry of Agriculture accused Ada Cole – and by association, the RSPCA – of having paid a Belgian butcher by the name of Franz Kools of Willebroek to kill horses with a knife so that a faked film could be made. A certain Captain Gee, Conservative MP for Bosworth – who had been awarded the VC at the Battle of Cambrai – stated publicly in the House of Commons that he could provide signed affidavits from Belgian butchers confirming that this was the case.

The RSPCA were appalled. Ada Cole had embarrassed them and, to make matters worse, as a direct result a Bill to prevent the export of horses which she and they had laid before Parliament had had to be abandoned.

But Ada Cole rejected the allegations out of hand, arguing that although she was a woman of strong convictions she would never resort to dishonest means to have them accepted. She challenged Captain Gee to produce his evidence. When he failed to do so, suddenly the focus of doubt shifted. The Ministry of Agriculture was likewise challenged to produce the affidavits, and likewise declined.

It began to look very much like a put-up job. The export of horses for butchery was a highly profitable business, and there were substantial vested interests that had a large stake in ensuring its survival.

But damage had been done both to the RSPCA and to Ada Cole, exacerbated by disagreements within the RSPCA Council. Despite her insistence that she could prove beyond doubt that the allegations were groundless, the Council issued a gagging writ against her and the Departmental Report stood intact.

The Captain, in the meantime, had disappeared. Some time later, from Australia, he sent an official apology which was read in the House of Commons, withdrawing all his allegations against Ada Cole and the RSPCA. The best that can be said of this sorry episode is that it attracted attention to the cause: everyone had their own view of the case, and the failure of the accusers to produce their evidence, along with the mysterious absence of Captain Gee, confirmed in most people's minds what had happened.

In 1926, the year of the General Strike, Ada Cole was given three months' salary in lieu of notice by the RSPCA and was offered a donation of £200 – no mean sum in those days – to continue her 'noble work under her own responsibility'.

Invited to remain in the RSPCA building and work from a small office there, she refused. She was not loved within the organization; for her part she had no time for its bureaucracy, its procedural delays or for any argument that did not relate directly to what she was doing. Her every comment to Council was prefaced by the phrase 'For the sake of the horses . . .' She set up instead in a small office in 11 Lincoln's Inn Fields, which she shared with Quakers.

Now she was fighting not just for her constant ends but for the very survival of her campaign. The government, in allowing the Report of the Departmental Committee to stand, had completely whitewashed the traffic in live horses. But she was not to be browbeaten. She was not interested in position, was incorruptible, independent and single-minded, in possession of hard evidence and now also in possession of influential friends.

During the post-war years another society had grown up, independent of the RSPCA and Ada Cole's Old Horse Traffic Committee, as she then called it. Known at first as the National Council Against the Export of Horses for Butchery, and subsequently as the National Council for Animal Welfare, it was formed in Lady Simeon's house in Wilton Crescent. Its members included Mr and Mrs Roper-Lumley-Holland, who held garden parties and social events to draw attention to the evils of the horse traffic, and Ada Cole was invited to these to speak.

It is difficult to imagine how she must have felt about another organization in her own field; yet these people had the money and social influence she needed, and eventually the National Council merged with her own society, adding their persuasive power to hers.

In 1927, the year before *Lady Chatterley's Lover* was first published, and a year after the first Mickey Mouse cartoon was screened, the Old Horse Traffic Committee officially became the International League Against the Export of Horses for Butchery, abbreviated to ILaEHB.

Beside Ada Cole now stood Lord Lambourne; Nina, Duchess of Hamilton; Emily Lind-af-Hageby; Mrs Roper-Lumley-Holland and Lady Simeon. She had met John Buchan, and knew John Galsworthy, who was chairman of the National Council for Animal Welfare; and was supported by the mercurial Annie Besant of the Theosophical Society. There were others.

The struggle for legislation continued. The Exportation and Transit of Horses, Asses and Mules Order had been passed in 1921. This was intended to improve conditions on shipboard for animals bound for slaughter, which were now supposed to be given adequate water and feed.

Ada Cole tried to bring in her own Bill, which was laid again before Parliament. At the same time the RSPCA supplied fourteen humane killers to Vaugirard, and the government, in view of this, rejected her Bill, arguing that since humane killers had been provided, the problem no longer existed.

But she knew every brick in Vaugirard and knew that the slaughtermen would no more use humane killers than give up butchering horses. Besides, her argument had not been that simple. She had argued for a cessation of the traffic not only because continental slaughterhouses were barbaric but because the whole system needed reviewing, and the very idea of transporting live animals for slaughter was offensive.

She was exhausted, and beaten by the RSPCA, on whose Council she had sat since 1928. On 17 July 1930, she made a speech to the Council which was ruled out of order, and on 16 October 1930, she attended her last Council meeting.

On the next day, 17 October 1930, in her room beside her office, she died at the age of seventy.

Lady Simeon wrote in *The Times*:

The death of Miss Cole has deprived the animal world, and especially its horses, of their most dauntless friend – one who was armed at every point with practical and expert knowledge of the work she undertook for them and who literally shared in some of their hardships, crossing the sea with them, and following them all along the road when they were disembarked. As a pioneer in the movement for saving the horses who had worked for us at home from being shipped abroad under terrible conditions, Miss Cole's name should ever be honoured.

It is indeed sad that she had not lived to see its fullest accomplishment in the passing of legislation which will abolish, without leaving any loophole, a traffic in horses sent abroad for butchery, or for a little more work before butchery, which public feeling in this country is unanimous in condemning. Those who knew what her work had been and that health and family life would have been sacrificed to it deeply hope that the memorial to her will be the one for which she strove in her last months, the passing of the Bill, Mr Ammons's and later taken over by Mr Broad, which the RSPCA and Animal Welfare Group of MPs –

formerly Sir Robert Gower, chairman of the RSPCA – have fathered.

That Miss Cole had faults which often made her not easy to work with her best friends will admit.

But they were most emphatically *les défauts de ses qualités* which made her intolerant of shams and misrepresentations which she felt were misleading the public and holding up her work.

Ada Cole was cremated in Golders Green Crematorium and her ashes scattered in the Garden of Remembrance.

She left behind to continue her work a young woman of twenty-one, named Sadie Baum.

THREE

In 1927, the eighteen-year-old Sadie Baum – as she was known
then – was shown into the cramped quarters of 11 Lincoln's Inn
Fields and introduced to Ada Cole by Violet English of the
National Council for Animal Welfare, who had taken a special
interest in Ada Cole's work and knew that she needed a secretary.

The tiny office contained only a typewriter and a few stacks of
pamphlets and address books. Sadie could type, but she had no other
experience and knew nothing about horses for slaughter or abattoirs
or what dreadful things they did in France. She hadn't had a chance to
find out about such things, she explained, on account of her age.

Ada Cole must have looked at her and wondered what to think.
A mere sixteen-year-old girl and all this!

And quite probably Sadie Baum wondered if she really wanted to
be connected with such grisly work, in spite of her own feelings
about animals. But something must have clicked, because she was
offered a temporary job 'for as long as the money lasts' and accepted
it.

She started straight away, pitched headlong into the Captain Gee
débâcle, thrown into the horse butchery business, plunged into con-
frontations with politicians and politics, attending meetings outside
and inside the House of Lords, taking minutes, and circulating posters, which she did on foot, trotting round London with them by the
armful.

At first it was just a job, but the job grew until she was working
non-stop – on part-time pay. And it grew from being a way of
earning money to a belief in a cause.

As her employer became weaker, so Sadie became not only
secretary but nurse, since Ada Cole was notoriously bad at feeding
herself and lived on a diet of biscuits, Jaffa oranges and boiled eggs.
Once she admitted to collapsing in a bath with a bottle of brandy to
help her feel better and joked about how she might appear to her

critics if one had chanced in and caught her lying in a tub of hot water the worse for wear with drink.

Sadie's space in the office was two shelves and a bookcase for the display of literature. She and Ada bought a duplicator to produce what became the first *Annual Report*, which was sent to members in England and contacts that had been established with like-minded individuals and societies throughout Europe. Ada Cole made a point of accepting help from any quarter, realizing that what she needed was membership and support from as far afield as possible.

Already there were people who were happy to follow her lead and became affiliated to her cause: people like Herr Von Braunbehrens and Justizrat Fraenkl in Berlin, whose office was as busy as its London counterpart, though independent of it and entirely self-supporting. The Berlin branch of the ILPH continued to run throughout the 1939–45 war, although for obvious reasons their records did not appear in the ILPH *Annual Reports*. But the moment the war ended, up they popped again, their links with London as close as ever.

Similar contacts were up and running by the thirties in France, in the Channel Islands, in Scotland and Ireland.

Sadie Baum was a very remarkable young girl.

When she began her work with Ada Cole they had a bank balance of £600. Three years later when Ada Cole died it was £965. 10s. 10d. The total asset value of the League was £1,400. 1s. 11d., including office furniture bought from bankrupt stock – £50 worth – and land bought for £371 in Bourne, Lincolnshire, on which stood Klondike Abattoir, set up by Ada Cole as a model where horses could be humanely slaughtered. There were 352 members, and Sadie was the only employee.

In her last year Ada Cole handed the greater part of the work over to Sadie Baum, or Anne Colvin, as we know her today. And what Anne Colvin had that Ada Cole lacked were the dual abilities of methodical organization, and the ability to get on with people from any walk of life. She took to heart the nature of the work and even at her young age managed to get people not only to listen to her but also to take her seriously.

She had a clear view of the way forward and knew that the only way to get things done was to attract into the League people who had clout, both political and social. She must have been a remarkably good judge of character, because she gathered round her a team who were to have real impact.

Geoffrey Gilbey, racing correspondent for the *Daily Express*, had had a letter published in the paper about the fate of workhorses for export which caused a storm of indignation. Anne Colvin was quick to seize this opportunity and asked him to become the first Chairman of the League, an invitation he immediately accepted.

Her Honorary Director was Brigadier General Sir George Cockerill, who resigned his seat in Parliament to take up the work of the League and was to remain with it until his death in 1957.

The first Treasurer was Ernest Bell, of Bell Publishing, and the President, Jules Rhul, who had walked with Ada Cole and the condemned horses on their ghastly journeys through the streets of Antwerp. The list of Patrons included Viscountess Bertie of Thame; Rt. Hon. Sir Arthur Griffith Boscawen, Minister of Agriculture in Ramsay MacDonald's Labour Government; Lady Constance Gore; Commentador Leonard Hawksley; Frances Countess of Warwick, and Lord and Lady Wharton. Their parliamentary secretary was the Hon. Elizabeth Kemeys-Tynte.

Anne Colvin was not slow to realize, in Sir George Cockerill's words, that 'social functions are good levers for popularizing and increasing membership of the League'. And it was numbers they were after, to help gain weight, power and credence. Thus in the 1930s social events were used as a platform for the ILPH to raise its profile and to gain popularity not only with the public but also with the press. For several years an Annual Horseshoe Ball was held at the Dorchester Hotel; these were glittering affairs attracting many society figures.

But what Anne Colvin would not tolerate were those who wanted to use the League as a means of social eventing and nothing else. What was important was the work. The whole thrust of the League was in the interest of horse welfare and horse welfare alone.

The main burden fell to her, and she worked from eight in the morning until ten or eleven at night, typing and circulating information often by hand and completely on her own initiative.

*

She did not suffer fools gladly. I have read some of her correspondence and one or two of her letters can be pretty sharp. Her family are revealing about her, particularly Alan Colvin, her son, who is a distinguished member of the ILPH Council today. Alan talked about his childhood and how he would often be kept awake as a little boy by the sound of a typewriter bashing away at two in the morning year after year. How when they went on holidays as a family, he remembers sitting on beaches while his mother wrote endless postcards to members of the ILPH, and how she engineered to be with interesting people and how nothing stopped her. He said that everyone they met was seen by his mother as a potential League member and that, on Flag Days, she managed to raise more money than anyone else because, to use his words, 'she could charm the birds off the trees'. For Anne, the day's work was never done and it is largely due to her that the ILPH is what it is today. She invested it with energy and singleness of purpose and peopled it with ability and skill. Among those she introduced into it was her own cousin Kay Colvin, who led it after Sir George Cockerill died, and her husband Mark, who was renowned for his command of English and for his financial wizardry when the going got tough. Her two sons sat on the Council, as did Stella Baum, her sister-in-law, who was employed by the ILPH in 1972, and still sits on the Council with Anne's son Alan today.

For her efforts she was awarded the MBE by Her Majesty The Queen in 1955, and the citation in *The Times* read: 'The recognition of her years of work to secure fair play for horses has been described by a colleague as a fitting climax to the year which produced the Horse's Charter.' This refers to the introduction of the Slaughter of Animals Amendment Act 1954.

The debt the ILPH owes to Anne Colvin is immense.

When I met her in 1992, its asset value including its farms and capital equipment exceeded £15 million. It employed dozens of people, fielded some twenty-five inspectors throughout Britain and Europe, was running courses on farriery, nutrition and saddlery in different countries worldwide, had trekking centre approval schemes operating as far afield as New Zealand, had undercover agents at work in Eastern Europe and was providing bursaries, veterinary facilities and training courses. At home it had four farms which were rest and rehabilitation centres for work-worn and debilitated horses, and it had over a thousand horses out on loan in England and Europe. It was working all over the world, being called on by governments internationally to advise on problems involving horses. It had over 50,000 members, a membership which was expanding at a rate of 1,000 a month.

The 1930s were a time of world trade depression. France had exacted a price from Germany for war reparations, America was wallowing in slump and Britain was struggling to keep her Empire running.

The music of Scott Joplin and Ragtime gave way to the bands of Glenn Miller and his emulators and George Formby strummed his ukulele in the dancehalls.

In Germany the Nazi Party was up, running and roaming the streets. On the night of 9 November 1938, Goebbels' brutes carried out their *Kristallnacht* horrors, and the writing was already on the wall. Incredibly, at the same time in Germany laws were enacted compelling all animal welfare societies to amalgamate so that no town had more than one. In Berlin the ILPH amalgamated with an organization called Deutsche Tierschutzverein, just as another law was brought in which punished cruelty to animals so severely that any overt acts of cruelty became a thing of the past. The few horses there were on the streets of Berlin were better treated than ever before, which prompted Sir George Cockerill to write with characteristic pith that 'in respect of the treatment of horses, conditions in Germany do, in fact, give cause for satisfaction'.

In 1937, after Sir George Cockerill's Exportation of Horses Act had put a ban on the trade in live horses for slaughter, the International League Against the Export of Horses for Butchery changed its name to the International League for the Protection of Horses.

Its popularity continued to grow. Within the next few years autonomous branches sprang up all over the country. They were all the more necessary since as it was now illegal to export horses for slaughter, and further mechanization was driving more horses off the land, there was a steady increase in unwanted workhorses for sale. Cases of abandonment became more common.

The branches were self-supporting. Their main function was to buy up old horses to prevent their falling into unscrupulous hands or dying of neglect. The prices paid for horses then seem amazing now. Miss Netta Ivory of the Scottish branch, in a period of one month, bought sixty-two horses at an average price of a guinea apiece. Horses were selling from the railway companies at between three and five pounds each, although some companies were more concerned about the fate of their old shunting horses than others, and refused to sell them through auction rooms. There were just too many horses for too few buyers and keeping them was costly.

In the mid-thirties too, the National Council for Animal Welfare amalgamated with the International League for the Protection of Horses. Their councils merged, their funds merged, and the two organizations, whose aims were to all intents and purposes identical, became a single, united force.

Altogether, the 1930s were a time not only of expansion but of consolidation for the ILPH. The League, it seemed, had not only arrived, but was here to stay.

Among those who were attracted to the ILPH in the 1930s was Freddy Fox, a top jockey of the day. Passionately interested in horse welfare, he had given an address at the Eccentrics Club on the export of horses for butchery, which prompted George Cockerill to write to him. Immediately convinced by Sir George's drive and sincerity and by the merits of the Bill he had drafted, later to become the Exportation of Horses Act 1937, Fox abandoned his plans for a society of his own, and decided instead to throw his weight behind the ILaEHB.

In an article headed 'Common Sense and the Work Horse' he wrote:

My experience has been that no movement which loses its head and indulges in vague idealism ever gets anywhere. For this reason I welcome every opportunity of explaining just what the International League for Horses seeks to do and why. This organisation is not a collection of cranks and old women, but a body composed of people who have practical experience of horses and who have examined the question from the economic as well as the moral point of view.

Freddy Fox had an enormous following. That he threw in with the ILaEHB gave it tremendous credence in the eyes of the racing world, which circle they had not yet penetrated.

A bust of Freddy Fox now stands in an alcove in the Head Office of the ILPH in Snetterton, though I daresay few of those who pass it know much about him.

Jean McDougall, who has been a member of the Council of the ILPH for a long time now – in fact she is its longest-serving member – met him back in the thirties. When I visited her at her home in Oxfordshire, in her sitting-room were photographs of her as a little girl in the company of the King of England, who shot with her father on the family estate in Scotland.

'My parents would have had fifty fits if they knew,' she smiled, taking a silver-handled riding whip off its place on the wall. I read the engraving: 'With love to Jean. From Freddy. 1935.'

Another leading light of the horse welfare world who was closely involved with the ILaEHB during these years was Dorothy Brooke, who was much admired for her work with the cavalry horses that had been left in Egypt following the end of the First World War. Her diaries, edited by Glenda Spooner, make moving reading. 'Old Bill', she wrote of one horse,

was without exception the most dreadful looking horse I have ever seen in my life. I have since dealt with hundreds as bad as he was, and some even worse, but he was my very first. I shall never forget the shock he gave me. I stood staring at him. Heavens knows the other horses were bad enough but somehow he was different. Obviously he had been a good horse once. He had been happy and well fed as the other poor animals had been. He had been born in England; he had known our green fields, been groomed and cared for. He had moreover served in Palestine and suffered hardships in that campaign as few horses have endured in modern times. And then we sold him to this.

She asked a Syrian who was looking at the horse with her what would become of him. He told her he would be treated for lameness then sent back to work. 'But he is completely worn out!' she protested. 'He is old,' the Syrian countered, 'and the Board wouldn't pass him for destruction. They have to be worse than that. He can get along when he is sound.'

She could not bear the thought of him returning to work, so she offered the going rate, which was nine pounds, though she had to wait a couple of days before the owner would accept it. In the two days she kept the horse he refused everything. He was past enjoyment. He refused bran treats, and the deep straw she gave him to lie on didn't interest him. He asked for nothing. There is little as pathetic in an old animal as his passive resignation to fate. As soon as he was hers, she had put him down.

Both Dorothy Brooke and her husband Geoffrey became members of the ILPH Council and for some years Anne Colvin acted as secretary for the Old War Horse Memorial Hospital, known today as the Brooke Hospital (Cairo). In 1932, Colonel Thomas Moore MP – later Chairman of the ILPH – brought the attention of the House of Commons to the plight of the war horses in Cairo on Dorothy Brooke's behalf, and in the same year proceeds from the Horseshoe Ball in the Dorchester were divided equally between the two charities.

Another great character was Bay de Courcy Parry, or Dalesman, as he was known to readers of *Horse and Hound*. There is a fund of stories about him: returning home from a day's hunting he called at the local pub for a drink only to be told that the place was shut.

'Where can I get a drink, then?' he called from the back of his hunter.

'Down the valley in Newcastle-on-Clun, The Crown.'

The Crown was four miles' hack. It was raining.

'That is,' the voice went on, 'unless you want to buy this place?'

'Buy it?' Bay called back.

'Buy it, and you can have your drink.'

'How much?'

'Seven hundred and fifty quid!' came the reply.

After a few moments' silence, a cheque for the same slipped beneath the door, and Bay got his drink.

He had bought The Anchor Inn, Kerry, Powys, where he lived for many years.

He took to the cause of work-worn horses as few others had, setting up something called the Dalesman Fund, which, although it operated outside the ambit of the League, saved hundreds of horses from export, and hundreds more from abandonment and a miserable end. And whether one likes or dislikes hunting is a matter of individual conscience and not a fitting subject for this book, but that men like de Courcy Parry should show such compassion to their own and other people's horses leaves one in little doubt as to the quality of the man he must have been.

FOUR

O f all the figures of the early days of the ILPH the most outstanding was Sir George Cockerill.

His entry in *Who's Who* is impressive. In 1892 he mapped the East Hindu Kush, and discovered Mount Dastoghil. He fought in the Boer War, and in the First World War worked in Military Intelligence. He was Member of Parliament for Reigate. He was Vice-President of The Poetry Society: he himself wrote sonnets – several of which were dedicated to Ada Cole – and a number of books, among them *Love's Universe*, *What Fools We Were* and *Late Harvest*.

But his genius was for legislation. It was he who drafted and pushed through Parliament all the major legislation for which the ILPH was responsible from 1937 until his death twenty years later at the age of ninety.

The Exportation of Horses Act, which finally became law in 1937, was a milestone in the history of the ILPH. It achieved everything Ada Cole had fought for. It prevented the export for slaughter of any horse under a certain value. This was the key, securing a measure of protection for all horses at risk, and is the basis for all the subsequent Minimum Values legislation which is still so vital today.

No sooner had the Exportation of Horses Act received Royal Assent, than Sir George Cockerill was asked to draft another Bill, which was to have equally important consequences for the horses of Britain.

A huge number of riding clubs and schools had sprung up all over Britain during the past few years because of a new interest in riding and trekking holidays. This was partly on account of A. F. Tschiffely who, in 1926, rode the ten thousand miles from Argentina to Washington DC. His journey took him two years and the book that followed, *Tschiffely's Ride*, became a bestseller.

In the thirties the thrill of Tschiffely's horseback adventures was fresh in people's minds and trekking became popular, its spread made easier by the kind of prices that were being paid for horses. Most of the new riding establishments were, however, lamentably short of management skills.

Sir Fred Hobday, Council Member of the ILPH, observed that 'the owners of these so-called Riding Schools do not know even the rudiments of feeding and stable management. In addition, the place of the good old-style groom who knew and loved his horses is nowadays often taken by a semi-scholarly amateur whose knowledge of stable hygiene and management of the saddle-room and its equipage is deplorable.

'Unfortunately, it is the poor beast which bears the brunt of it all.'

In an open letter to *The Times*, Sir George put forward the bones of his new Bill, which was to lay down the standard of care which all establishments offering horses for hire should maintain. This had the approval of the RSPCA and the support of Our Dumb Friends League, both of whom worked harmoniously with the ILPH to ensure that the Bill became law.

The Riding Establishment Act received Royal Assent on 28 July 1939 – a date which marked a six-year interruption in Sir George's legislative programme.

Five weeks later, Hitler invaded Poland.

The minutes of the ILPH Council for 1943 read as follows:

The last Council Meeting was held on Tuesday, 23 July 1940, when the next meeting was arranged for 22 October. Between those dates, however, much happened. On 8 August the first of the four phases of the Battle of Britain began. On that day and on 12 August, 182 German planes were destroyed. On the 13th and 14th, 110 suffered the same fate, and on the 15th, 180 more.

Between the 16th and 18th, 225 were shot down – a total of 697 enemy planes against 153 of ours, of which the pilots of no less than 60 were safe. There was a quiet day on 18 August.

The second phase is reckoned to have begun on 19 August. Actually, the enemy was refuelling until the 24th, when his attack began again. Between 19 August and 5 September he lost 562 planes to our 219, out of which 132 pilots were safe.

The third phase began on 6 September. On this occasion London was the enemy's main objective. On the 10th, a sub-committee of the ILPH was held at 19, Knightsbridge, and on that day air-raids were practically continuous from midday until 4.30 a.m. the following morning. The climax of the attack came on the 15th, when the enemy lost 185 out of 500 planes over London.

In the fourth phase the enemy used only fighters and fighter bombers. The Battle of Britain is officially reckoned to have ended on 31 October, and, in the 85 days that it lasted, 2,375 enemy planes were destroyed.

It will be appreciated that it would have been difficult to hold our 22nd meeting on that fixed date. Few, except those whose duty enforced their stay in London, remained. Many of the Council had felt it right to leave and the restriction of the travelling facilities made their return as difficult as it was undesirable.

In the same year the *Annual Report* reads:

It is clear from the correspondence we receive on the subject of war horses that there is acute anxiety in the mind of the public lest our horses should suffer the same fate as befell their predecessors at the close of war. It seems, therefore, desirable to repeat that we have absolute assurance from the Secretary of State for War that in no circumstances would our horses be sold overseas, that every possible provision is being made for their welfare and well-being, and that British Army horses on foreign service would either be brought back to the United Kingdom or be humanely destroyed abroad under military supervision.

Similar assurances were received from General Sir Archibald Wavell (as he was then), Commander of Imperial Forces in the Middle East, concerning the huge contingent of horses deployed there.

The German Cavalry were as concerned about the fate of their horses as the British were about theirs. After the war an extraordinary account came to light. On 8 May 1944, Hitler had ordered a unit of the 17th Army to evacuate the Crimea and have their entire stock of 30,000 horses shot. The troops refused. These men had ridden a long way on these horses and would not be so lightly treated: they were tough and proud cavalrymen.

The Veterinary Corps were then ordered on pain of execution to shoot the horses since the men had refused, and one by one the horses were led off, shot and thrown over the cliffs into the sea. By afternoon the scene of execution was ankle deep in blood, and since time was running out, the remaining horses were herded together and machine-gunned in a barrage of continuous fire until not one remained.

The sea heaved in hideous carnage for months following.

The aftermath of the 1939–45 war in England meant rationing and paper shortages while the black marketeers were having a high time of things, as they ever will. George Formby's ukulele had given way to the lyrics of Cole Porter. The crooners Perry Como and Frank Sinatra were beginning to make a name for themselves and the Ink Spots came over from America. In the tail-end of the forties, Bing Crosby sang his way through a million perennial White Christmases and still does.

There was a story for everything.

Stories of human courage, the dogged determination of those who survived the death camps and the darkness of the Hitler years. There were stories of men dying, and of men being saved, stories of women who gave their all to save their countrymen, and of those who betrayed them.

And there were stories about animals: remarkable stories. I recall one from the Mounted Branch of the Manchester police of a horse who not only once, but twice booted an incendiary bomb out of his locked stable, taking with it the door and certain death.

The ILPH suffered losses of its own.

Freddy Fox was killed in a car crash. It was a severe blow. His contribution had been immense. He helped with technical information, he helped in disputes about horses in work, those fit for work, or those not. He wrote letters to the press and kept the public constantly in touch with events involving horses even in the darkest days of the war. He helped to oversee the running of Klondike Abattoir, which during the war put down more horses than ever before, since demand for food meant that the consumption of horsemeat increased dramatically. When old or cast horses were sent there, they were given a field, and water, and shelter and stables – everything they needed. When their time had come, they died with mouths full of carrots.

Freddy Fox used to pay surprise visits to Klondike and always found it to be as he wished: clean, and bloodless. After each horse was killed, the floor was washed down so that the next horse would be spared as much trauma as possible and put down in complete ignorance of his own demise.

A couple of days before his death, Freddy Fox wrote to George Cockerill:

It is very hard for some people to sign an old friend's death warrant. I have an old horse called Tim I have hunted fifteen seasons before the war, and he will be 28 on 1 January. He is turned out rough in my orchard here with a box to go into if he likes, with a small feed at night and morning and an armful of hay. I have a hack round when time permits, and one of us has a word for him every day, so he is alright and looks it. But his time will come and you have no idea how much even the thought of it haunts me. I have seen old favourites pensioned off miles from anywhere, nobody going near them for days, weeks or months, no shelter, nothing but winter picking to eat in winter months. Horses, I am sure, love human companionship, and owners who are only putting off for a year or two what has to be done eventually may be causing dreadful suffering by mistaken kindness ... if this, my letter serves to point this out to only a few of the thoughtless or uninitiated, it will have been worthwhile.

Freddy Fox died thirteen days before Christmas 1945. From the day of his death, his 'closest silent pal', old Tim, would not eat. Tim never saw his twenty-eighth birthday.

And another long-standing member of the Council died. Captain Parsons, who ran ILPH Jersey, was imprisoned by the Germans during the occupation of the island. He escaped to England but died later in hospital of exposure. Lest he fall into the wrong hands, Captain Parsons shot his horse before he left.

*

No sooner was the war over than George Cockerill resumed his tireless efforts to protect horses by means of proper legislation. In the post-war world, fired with enthusiasm for a new beginning, the ILPH had great plans. In the 1950s there came a whole spate of Acts which, when they were not entirely drafted by members of the League, had the benefit of ILPH research, advice and support.

The first problem to be addressed was the system of minimum values, which by now was in need of revision. By the end of the war the price of horses in England had risen rapidly. The minimum value laid down by the 1937 Act – £25 per horse – below which an animal could not be exported, was now too low to prevent the sale of live horses for meat, and the export trade had begun afresh as a result.

The ILPH had foreseen this problem, and the 1937 Act did in fact include provision for the values to be increased, as Sir George reminded the Minister of Agriculture in 1949: '... in 1937 the amounts were quite adequate to prevent the export of horses for butchery, with its inevitable cruelties, which was this League's main interest in the matter. But it was realised that this would not always be the case, and so we inserted a clause giving the Minister of Agriculture power to vary the values as ... necessary.'

Sir George's letter urged the Minister that the time was ripe to increase the values. A Committee of Enquiry into the Export and Slaughter of Horses was set up under Lord Rosebery, and in 1950 the amended Exportation of Horses (Minimum Values) Act was incorporated into the major Diseases of Animals Act which consolidated the previous legislation, among it the original Exportation of Horses Act of 1937.

The year before, 1949, the Riding Establishments Act had been amended, on ILPH advice, to include a clause to ensure that all commercial stables should be properly registered and inspected.

In 1952 came the Horses (Sea Transport) Order, which laid down the conditions under which horses could be carried at sea.

The Slaughter of Animals (Amendment) Act and the Slaughter of Animals (Prevention of Cruelty) No. 2 Regulation both came into force in 1954, and between them laid down standards of hygiene, treatment of animals on slaughterhouse premises and humane methods of dispatch. They also implemented suggestions made jointly by George Cockerill and Lord Merthyr, Chairman of the RSPCA, that one Ministry should be responsible for all matters to do with slaughterhouses and knackers' yards, and that all horses the flesh of which was intended for human consumption should be slaughtered in government-licensed abattoirs. For the first time in England, slaughterhouses were brought under government control.

In 1954, too, the ILPH obtained the Horses (Landing from Northern Ireland and the Republic of Ireland) Order, which went some way towards protecting horses imported across the Irish Sea to Britain from unnecessary suffering during transit.

And all this when George Cockerill was well into his eighties – in this busiest of years, 1954, he was eighty-seven years old.

It was George Cockerill who drew up the first official Deed of Declaration of Trust of the ILPH, which was made on 20 May 1952. This document laid down formally the scope of the ILPH's activities, its aims, its constitution, and the powers and responsibilities of its trustees.

The Declaration of Trust Deed today (see Appendix 2) is rather different from its predecessor, but then the aims and activities of the ILPH have changed in order to meet the challenges of the modern world.

George Cockerill died in 1957, still active at the age of ninety. He left a void the ILPH found it very hard to fill. Lt. Col. Viscount Elibank wrote:

> We met after I had entered the House of Commons. Sir George Cockerill was at that time serving in the War Office, but our paths crossed on the subject of the abominable traffic in poor worn-out horses to the Continent. I came to know Sir George well and to appreciate to the full his qualities of kindliness, steadfastness of purpose, and ardent sense of justice for his fellow creatures and for dumb animals unable to plead for themselves. In no field was this latter quality more persistently and successfully displayed than in campaigns to mitigate the evils of the trade in old horses . . .

Many other tributes left no doubt of the esteem in which he was held. But there can be no better epitaph than one of his own sonnets.

Whose is the right to live? Each holds in trust
To be in loving service richly spent
The current coin in which his loaned dust
Is minted in God's image. Discontent
Rifles his store, whose hoarded happiness
Is not twice blessed. To love and serve must be
Both end and means whereby man may express
His inescapable divinity.
His life rings true who consecrates his strength,
Time, talent, vision, sympathy and skill
In fealty to his fellows. Thus at length
He may redeem his loan, himself fulfil.
He lives who serves. Who serves must surely keep
Watch o'er himself, ward o'er his Master's sheep.

PART THREE

Changing Times: Into the Modern Era

FIVE

Ada Cole had cherished a dream of a rest home where old and work-worn horses could end their days in comfort before they were slaughtered. Ideally, she said, she would have liked to have seen such centres all over England, but she would have been happy for the League to have established just one.

She did not live to see it. One month after her death, however, in November 1930, her friend and colleague Dr Rose Turner proposed to the Council of the ILaEHB that 'we should rent a field, buy in old horses, keep them a day or two, and have two women attendants who will witness the humane putting down . . .'

Her plan was accepted: it would be an ideal memorial to the founder of the League. A legacy of £500 was donated for its establishment, and notification of the new Memorial Stables was sent out to 10,000 subscribers. At 3.30 p.m. on 11 May 1932, the Ada Cole Memorial Stables, built on eight-and-a-half acres of land at South Mimms, Hertfordshire, were opened by Her Grace Nina, Duchess of Hamilton. Their first occupant was Gunner, an old bay hunter who had belonged to the remount officers in the First World War, and had seen action at Gallipoli.

Before long, the condition of the horses that the Stables took in improved so greatly as a result of the care and attention they received that it became folly to have them slaughtered. Accordingly, the first loan scheme was developed, under which heavy horses were loaned to firms for draught work on the strict understanding that the staff of the Memorial Stables should have access to them at any time, in order to inspect the conditions in which they were kept and satisfy themselves as to the standard of their care.

A similar kind of loan scheme – though now generally for riding horses – still operates today.

*

In 1932, Sir George Cockerill, his time and energy fully occupied with the thorny problems of legislation, handed over the responsibility for the Ada Cole Memorial Stables to Dr Turner, and despite the opposition of Anne Colvin, Dr Turner's proposal that the Stables should be run as a separate entity, with its own Council, executive and staff, was carried.

Only ever intended by the Executive Committee of the League as a temporary expedient, the split proved irreversible. The successful and newly independent Stables showed little inclination to return to its parent body, and in spite of attempts to reunite the two in 1948 and again in 1987, the Ada Cole Memorial Stables and the ILPH have remained separate ever since. The irony was not lost on the ILPH, whose *Annual Report* for 1947 reads, 'It was never intended that the separation should be permanent, but, unfortunately, the creation of an independent Council for the Stables has had that effect and every effort to induce it to return to its former allegiance has failed. Thus, the curious anomaly exists that the Ada Cole Memorial Stables, built and endowed by the International League as a memorial to its Founder, disclaim any connection with the parent body while clinging to its Founder's name.'

And yet, it must be immediately apparent to anyone who visits either the ILPH or the Ada Cole Memorial Stables that the two charities remain united, at least in some sense, by their common beliefs and their common aims. Today, the Ada Cole Memorial Stables occupies forty-five acres of lush green pasture between the hamlet of Broadley Common and Harlow New Town, Essex, and is home to a large number of previously neglected or otherwise distressed horses, ponies and donkeys. It is a rescue centre rather than a retirement home: horses are rehabilitated here, and after a period of convalescence, or whatever the particular horse requires, they are found foster homes, although they will always belong to the Ada Cole Stables.

Director of the Stables now is Eric Collier. He has a colourful background: having seen service with the RAF in the Far East, he trooped the bush on horseback in Southern Rhodesia – now Zimbabwe – as a member of the Rhodesian Police, before turning to commerce to become a top executive with the Zimbabwe Cotton

Marketing Board. He runs a fine yard, and the Stables are a joy to visit. I reckon Eric must be as tough as the horses he trooped the Rhodesian bush on, because the day I met him he'd lost a finger in one of those lightning accidents that happen with ropes and horses, and though he was one digit short he chatted on about the horses and the yard as though nothing had happened, save making some remark about finding it a nuisance having to dream up new ways of holding a cup of coffee.

The ILPH may have lost the Ada Cole Memorial Stables, but it did not lose sight of Ada Cole's dream, and in 1948 it was finally fulfilled with the purchase of Cherry Tree Farm in Newchapel, near Lingfield, Surrey.

The Council of the ILPH saw in Cherry Tree a place that would be the tangible heart of their work, the embodiment of their philosophy, a place where they could see directly the results of what they did; where they and their visitors could see the old, tired horses they had rescued thrive and blossom under their care.

There were doubts at first: when they bought it, it was an inch short of a ruin. Had they done the right thing? Who would run it? Would they find the horses to stock it? They need not have worried. Cherry Tree Farm proved an immediate success, and within a very short time had deservedly become the apple of the ILPH's eye.

The first manager of the farm was Harry Hardaker, who moved in with his wife on St Francis Day, 4 October 1948, bringing with them their very first charge, an emaciated little tinker's pony called Caravan. Caravan was followed by Snowball and Beauty, both bought from an horrific slaughterhouse which the ILPH had had shut down. Then came costermongers' horses, totters' horses, heavy horses, police horses, circus horses, gypsy horses; racehorses, hunters, hacks, ponies and donkeys. By the time the farm had been established for a few years, in the mid-fifties, they had received literally thousands of requests to take in unwanted horses. Among them were Charlie, the very last railway horse to work in England, and a horse called Bondsman which Geoffrey Gilbey had bought at auction. Geoffrey Gilbey knew his horses. He had seen this one run in the 1934 Derby, and knew also that he had been General

Eisenhower's hack during the war. He bought him for his meat price, and Bondsman ended his days happily, cropping grass in oak-fringed paddocks.

Cherry Tree Farm was officially opened on 13 October 1949, an event which attracted considerable attention to the ILPH: articles appeared not only in their long-time supporters the *Manchester Guardian* and *The Times* but in newspapers as far afield as New Zealand, New York and Chicago. All the horses that were in residence at the time took part in the ceremony: Dolly and Dinkie and Prince and Ruelfa, Smokey and Strawberry and Pilot and Bunty and Heavens – why do horses wind up with such daft names? And there were wonderful stories. One is of a seventy-four-year-old farrier – compelled to leave his premises in the East End of London to make way for a high-rise block and anxious about the future of his horses Jim, Ada and John – who wrote to the Queen Mother. The story featured in the press and four days later the old man, red-eyed and wobbly chinned, accompanied his precious old horses to Cherry Tree, where he and his wife visited them every weekend to the end of their days.

Practical work was undertaken at Cherry Tree, too. They had a foal with a broken leg which the Royal Veterinary College set in fibreglass in one of the first experiments in this new material. After a month of intensive care at Cherry Tree, the splint was removed and the foal's leg found to be completely healed. Horses were used for all the field work on the farm and a pair of Shires, Lion and Violet, who had both come in as redundant horses, not only found themselves fully employed on the farm once more but went on to win ploughing competitions to boot.

Individual boxes in the stables were named after favourites long gone. One is dedicated to Jack, Santa Barbara, California, by a Mrs Ravenscroft in memory of her cherished pony who lived from 1900 to 1933. There is the Golden Miller box, dedicated to the matchless steeplechaser who won five consecutive Cheltenham Gold Cups between 1932 and 1936. And there is of course the Freddy Fox memorial box, opened in 1951 by Gordon Richards – later Sir Gordon – himself one of the greatest jockeys to ride in Britain in this or any previous century. On a wonderfully sunny day, a crowd of 500 attended and a Pathé film crew made a half-hour documentary under the title *Gordon Helps Old Horses*, which was screened in cinemas all over the country on 21, 22 and 23 June 1951. And among the celebrities who graced Cherry Tree with their presence was Sun Chariot, the greatest race mare ever to carry the royal colours, whom Gordon Richards had ridden to victory in the fillies' Triple Crown of 1942.

For some reason, in the 1950s and the early years of the 1960s, Cherry Tree Farm seemed to strike a chord in the mind of the British public.

It was a decade of tremendous change. The old King had died and a new young Queen was on the throne. Edmund Hillary and Sherpa Tenzing Norgay conquered Everest. Bands were playing the songs of Nat King Cole and the wilder sounds of Bill Haley and the Comets and Elvis Presley and his 'Blue Suede Shoes' filled the air-waves. The phenomenon of the teenager had begun. It was the era of the Suez Crisis, of the Korean War, the era that brought the world close to its demise with the proliferation of nuclear weapons, the Bay of Pigs and President Kennedy's final warning.

In the Soviet Union, Khrushchev's Virgin Lands policy drew collectives together into vast areas and changed the face of Central Asia, turning huge tracts of land to cotton production, the result of which was to drain the Oxus and turn the Aral Sea into a poisonous swamp. The word was mass collective production at any price and huge tracts of steppe went under the plough. It also meant that since the State was responsible for all agriculture, no man was allowed to own livestock privately, and thousands of horses went for slaughter. There is a gripping documentary about this in the hands of the Equine Institute in Moscow, and although the subject of the film, made by Turkmenian Television, is a race from Ashkhabad to Moscow on horseback– some 3,000 kilometres – it alludes power-fully to the fact that so many horses and bloodlines were lost during this period. Of course, the Russians acknowledge this and have very fine studs indeed today where breeding policies are once again in place – in Stavropol notably, and Piatigorsk, where you can visit an enormous selection of types such as we rarely see in England: hardy Kabardins, Tiersk, Karachai, Dons, Budyonnys and the beautiful Akhal Tekes, desert raiders' horses, fine and haughty, yet whose numbers rapidly declined in the late 1950s. Little of this came to light at the time, and it is only through the persistence and work of such authorities as Vivienne Burdon that we know more now about the variety and excellence of Russian breeds. Who knows how the genetic pool from which these breeds spring may one day benefit other horses round the world? This is a sphere, although it is early days yet, in which the ILPH is helping to build up a picture.

At the same time it was the beginning of the Space Race, of Sputniks – how many ponies I recall being named Sputnik I shall never know: 'sputnik', by the way, is Russian for travelling companion – and Yuri Gagarin's picture was everywhere: the first man in space. The Russians had won. It was a vibrant if uncertain era and threw the world headlong into an arms race and Cold War that led to Vietnam and all the horrors of that débâcle.

And yet, through all this, the simple, wholesome story of Cherry Tree Farm and its horses was one which touched people's hearts. Visitors came not only from all over England but from overseas as well; hundreds of them, young and old, with their sandwiches and dogs and treats for the horses: packets of mints and bags of apples. Perhaps, in an era of change and doubt, Cherry Tree's appeal was its message of peace and hope. It seems that it was not only a place of therapy for horses.

Altogether, the fifties were something of a golden age for the ILPH: seldom has its public profile been higher, or its work more widely known.

Meanwhile in England the great drift from the land was well under way, and with the horses went the men. I remember it personally. I remember a big bob-tailed old Shire called Flower, who lived in Kildane, a field at the bottom of a neighbouring farm. She was the charge of a man called Old Ashe Able. Flower and Old Ashe Able were friends to dozens of children who'd stand round Flower and listen to Ashe tell glowing stories about her, of her great strength and power; how she'd ploughed and harvested every field thereabouts since Noah was a lad. He'd take us for rides on her, four at a time, and afterwards we'd pat her huge flanks and feed her apples.

She was exchanged for a T20 Ferguson tractor. Old Ashe lost his job. For us children, life was never the same again. I don't know where she went. Old Ashe Able lived alone from then on in some dairy cottages and spent the rest of his life, which wasn't long, pinning beautifully scripted copperplate handwritten signs to gates: 'The Lord giveth and The Lord taketh away'.

But for hundreds of other horses made redundant, like Flower, from the land, Cherry Tree had come just in time. And not just for farm horses, either. Throughout the sixties and the seventies, the ILPH continued to take in horses from all walks of life. One such was Hercules. Everybody knew him; he had been in his day one of the most popular horses in England. You could watch him any Monday night slapping up the street in the East End of London, pulling his filthy old cart loaded with filthy old clothes, smelly old bones and useless household junk. Hercules featured in countless episodes of the hugely successful BBC classic comedy series, *Steptoe and Son*, until this scruffy, placid, unkempt old Dobbin retired after a lifetime's work to Cherry Tree Farm.

Several other ILPH Homes of Rest for Horses were opened after Cherry Tree. There was one for a time at Alkrington, Manchester. There was the Lady Grey Edgerton Home at Sidlesham, near Chichester, and the Wheal Ellen Home in Truro, both of which closed in the 1970s, and Little Church Farm at Wilstead in Bedfordshire, which ran until 1983. In 1962, Charles Bennington, later to become Director of the ILPH, loaned his home, Overa House Farm in Norfolk, for use as a home for rescued horses, a use in which it has continued to this day.

Today the ILPH has four farms where horses either live out their retirement or are rehabilitated and rehomed. In addition to Cherry Tree and Overa, there is Overa's near neighbour at Snetterton, Norfolk: Hall Farm, now the headquarters of the ILPH. Of the two Norfolk farms, Overa has the more cosy feel, largely because of its siting and its scale, its thatched farmhouse and quadrangle of looseboxes hemming flower beds and lawn. Somehow it is reminiscent of Cherry Tree. Hall Farm is different: it has an airier feel, and is grander altogether. It feels like HQ.

The fourth and newest farm is Belwade in Scotland, given to the

ILPH by Mrs Diana Elliot of Drumnagesk in 1989 and opened by HRH The Princess Royal in August 1990. Belwade is a wonderful place. It's about thirty miles from Aberdeen. To reach it you leave the main road and bump along a dirt track through whispy Scots birch woodland, and when I visited it in autumn the colours were at their best, with rowan berries hanging in brilliant red clusters, a sudden shock of crimson in the browns, silvers and bronzes, with the forest underworld deep green and mossy and full of rabbits.

Going down the drive you come across a 'wee little hoose' which is where Liz, one of the grooms lives, and then, past a stand of young shrubs planted by Hamish Lochore, you come on the farm itself, a great quadrangle of granite, like its surroundings, low in profile. The colour of the stone is comfortable in the landscape, in harmony with the delicate greys and pinks of the wintering trees. The forests opposite the farm are larch, and the hilltops are covered in bracken, which in autumn was a rich, rusty brown. The hills to the west were already snow-covered, and boded – so Eileen Gillen, manager of Belwade, felt – a long, cold spell. Down past the paddocks the River Dee sparkles in watery sunlight where it runs shallow over smooth pebbles. Between the river and the farm the horses graze: police horses, Shetlands, Highland ponies and others. They were well content.

Belwade has been extensively restored. There are twelve new looseboxes and three smaller stables. The original granite yard is now covered and makes a barn for hay, straw and the bales of Auboise or hemp, which is used for bedding. Liz Robertson, Sharon Ellis and Alec Cowe work with the horses, and Eileen Gillen, as well as managing the farm, understudies Hamish Lochore, who is ILPH Field Director for Scotland.

Hamish Lochore was in the Scots Greys with George Stephen, Chief Executive of the ILPH, and is something of an old chum. He's resoundingly good company even though you can hear him in the next county when he laughs; he lives in what he describes as 'a huge crumbling barrack of a place, moving from room to room, burning the furniture on the way'. He tells a good story and officiates at open days, both at Belwade and Hall Farm. One story he and Eileen told me between them, punctuated by irreverent chortling and a certain amount of embarrassed giggles. It was about Annabel, a very aged donkey who had won the affection of some children at the local school.

One day the children received a letter from the ILPH which their teacher decided to keep unopened until they were all assembled in the main hall. She thought she would surprise her pupils with a letter from Annabel, and make their day. The moment arrived, the children assembled, and the teacher opened the letter. It read: 'The ILPH regrets to inform her friends and admirers that Annabel the donkey died on the morning of . . .'

I'm ashamed to say I fell about laughing. Maybe it was the way that Eileen and Hamish told it. There are kinder Annabel stories, too. One wintry morning she was nowhere to be found, until Eileen looked out across the fields and saw in the distance two long donkey ears poking through a high white drift. It took four hours to dig her out. And before her death she lived a privileged life, visiting Balmoral on more than one occasion, where she received lumps of sugar from a royal hand.

While I was there, Eileen, Hamish and David Craig, ILPH field officer for the west of Scotland, were making preparations to remove the feral ponies from the island of Eigg. The ponies had been causing havoc in recent years, trampling crops and gardens, and many of the islanders had had enough. Some had even threatened to shoot them. It was not going to be easy. The ponies were all unbroken, and large – about fourteen hands apiece. There were no holding pens for them on the island, and the ferry only runs once a week. And if those difficulties were not enough, some people liked to have the ponies on the island, viewing them as an attraction, and objected to their removal in the first place.

Life at Belwade is a lot more than just fun and laughter.

And at the other end of the country, surrounded by the thick oak woods of Surrey the farm that began it all still thrives, its role as vital to the ILPH as it was when they first bought it over forty years ago. In its oak-railed paddocks are horses old and young, difficult horses, horses that lay down if you tried to mount them or put them in harness. There are horses that have been badly handled, whipped or maltreated, horses that have known terror and neglect; all there, glossy and contented, cropping the grass at Cherry Tree under the watchful eye of horsemaster and present manager Ian Gibbs, one of the longest-serving employees of the ILPH.

SIX

Of the early 1960s, what can I say? It was an exciting time to live through, an unforgettable, free-thinking time, vibrant and memorable – and chilling. The Beatles released their first hits – and in America on 22 November 1963 President John F. Kennedy was assassinated. I remember his funeral on television, and one particular powerful and haunting image: directly behind Kennedy's coffin, led by a soldier, there walked a single, riderless horse.

And though the sixties were a headlong, hedonistic age, it was also a time when the young began to take an interest in their environment as never before. Partly this stemmed from the ever-present threat of nuclear war, and from the early protest movements such as the Aldermaston marches. In any event, a real sense of responsibility for the planet and its inhabitants, both human and animal, seemed to grow out of a realization of what we had to lose. And the ILPH found a new and receptive climate for its work, a wider, more global outlook and a new way forward.

The *Annual Report* for the year 1961–2 gives the assets of the ILPH as some £165,000. Life membership cost ten guineas, and the subscription for annual members ten shillings. It ran three retirement and rehabilitation homes for horses: Cherry Tree, Little Church Farm in Bedford and Stepaside in Ireland. It was a healthy organization, ripe for an injection of new blood and new enthusiasm.

The man who led it into the modern era was Captain Charles Bennington. A life member of the ILPH in the fifties, in the sixties he worked in the capacity of Honorary Field Supervisor, becoming Honorary Director in 1972. But whatever his job title, Charles Bennington carved out for himself within the ILPH a role unlike any that had existed before.

His style differed from that of his predecessors. Until Bennington, the directors of the ILPH had been for the most part deskbound, brilliant communicators and diplomats whose skills had been to secure a measure of influence for the ILPH, to steer the legislation it sponsored through the appropriate channels, to keep the ILPH in the public eye.

Diplomatic Bennington was not. Effective he most certainly was. Bennington was what the Italians call *appassionato*. But his ideas and convictions, however passionate, sprang from sound practical experience. He was not apt to delegate: if something needed to be done, he would get stuck in and do it.

There is a story which tells how once, when a shipload of South American horses was due to land in Italy, the ILPH had been unable to establish whether they were due to dock at Genoa or Trieste. When Bennington, in Genoa, discovered it was to be Trieste, he chartered a small open-cockpit plane and flew it himself across Italy, landing, at night, as close to the docks as he was able. That was the sort of man he was.

I have heard all sorts of things said about Charles Bennington: how he could cut people dead and had no time for fools; how, as he got older, he grew deaf and became increasingly difficult to work with. He could be hard to know, cantankerous and sometimes plain unpleasant.

But he loved his horses. He had both a cavalry background and an intuitive flair for handling horses. He was a horseman with a capital H. He had vision, and complete dedication to his work; and his achievements speak for themselves.

It was Bennington who set up the system of field officers which forms the backbone of the ILPH's work today, and for this purpose he recruited men who were knowledgeable about horses, familiar with the law and used to handling people. He knew the kind of men he wanted, and he found them among the ranks of the mounted police.

Ron Jordan, field officer for Norfolk and East Anglia, who joined the ILPH in 1982, is just such a man. A member of the Metropolitan Police since 1948, he had risen to be a Chief Inspector of the mounted branch. Ron worked closely with Captain Bennington and was for a time, in practical terms, his second-in-command. Perhaps they got on so well because they shared a background not only in horses but in aviation, Ron having been a member of the Fleet Air Arm.

One day, Ron told me, he and Bennington had driven back to Overa House Farm – Bennington's home, which he leased to the ILPH in 1962 – all the way from Cornwall, where they had delivered a couple of horses. It had been a long trip and they had shared the driving. By the time they got back to base they had been on the road for fourteen hours, and Bennington went straight into the office to sort out paperwork for the following day.

Ron felt like nothing more than going home. But, being the fellow he is, he mucked out the horsebox and hosed it down. It was dark, and he was about all in.

He had just finished and was packing up to go home when Bennington appeared from the office. Ron said to him, 'Box is all cleaned out and hosed down ready for tomorrow.'

'And so it damn well should be!' Bennington snapped, and drove off.

Ron knew when not to be offended. Charles Bennington was a hard-headed, old-school horse-coper. When Ron got into his car he burst out laughing. After all, he asked himself, what had he expected him to say?

To someone who shouted back at him, when he had commented on their riding position, 'I have been riding for twenty-five years!' Bennington answered, 'Correction! You may have been sitting on horses for twenty-five years, but you have certainly not been riding!'

'You know,' concludes Ron, 'he was an irascible old sod: but I loved him.'

In 1966, when he was still Honorary Field Supervisor, Bennington toured Europe to see for himself the work which the ILPH could do there, and as a result of his trip a number of overseas projects were initiated in which, typically, he took a personal hand. In Greece, when he introduced humane killers to replace the primitive and barbaric methods of slaughter which had been in use, he himself demonstrated their operation. These Greener Humane Killers were distributed all over Europe, and even sent as far afield as Chile.

Yet, at the same time as he was running around the world, this extraordinary man still found the time to make miniature models of cavalry regiments, French, Polish, German, Boer and Indian: The Royal Horse Artillery Regiment – his own – The Royal Scots Greys of 1800, and even a young Winston. These were exhibited at Overa in a Museum of Equine Culture which he set up there, and which proved to be enormously popular with visitors.

The ILPH was busy on its home ground, too. Throughout the sixties and into the seventies it continued to sponsor and support legislation on behalf of Britain's horses. 1964 saw a new Riding Establishment Act, which was further improved and updated in 1970 to include provision for adult supervision of riders, restrictions on the use of pregnant mares, and proper indemnity against potential injury to clients.

1969 brought the Ponies Act, which closed an unfortunate loop-hole left by earlier legislation under which ponies, generally worth less than horses because of their smaller size, were inadequately protected. The new law laid down minimum values specifically for ponies, below which they could not be exported for slaughter: £40 for a Shetland, £70 for a pony up to twelve hands in height, and £100 for others.

And it was in the sixties that the ILPH first initiated a number of schemes and projects to improve aspects of horse care and manage-ment: schemes through which they forged links with other equestrian welfare bodies which are still maintained today.

In 1960, the first ILPH scholarship was awarded to enable selec-ted veterinary students to undertake specialized training or research. Resulting studies which have made valuable contributions to equine welfare include radiological techniques for the early diagnosis of lameness, and the effects of nutrition on the physiology of mares. In addition to their own scholarships, the ILPH provided financial assistance to other veterinary projects: ILPH funds contributed to the Veterinary Field Station of the Royal School of Veterinary Studies at Edinburgh University, and in 1969 an ILPH grant to the Univer-sity of Liverpool helped fund a study of the nutritional problems faced by the wild ponies of the New Forest. Since 1973 the ILPH has contributed to the work of the Equine Research Station at New-market, a world leader in its field, where vital and up-to-the-minute research is conducted into a whole range of equine diseases, illnesses and treatment.

At the same time, the ILPH set up farriery schemes – the first in 1960 – whereby contributions were made directly to the wages of approved apprentices. Good farriers were becoming hard to find, and the ILPH was concerned both to encourage newcomers into the trade and to ensure that standards were maintained. If there is one man who is more important to the well-being and health of the horse than the vet, that man is the farrier, as Xenophon understood over twenty-three centuries ago. Today, in the 1990s, farriery and its techniques play a vital part in the work of the ILPH all round the world.

Originally, the role of the farrier and that of the blacksmith had been quite distinct. The blacksmith was a worker in iron, a toolmaker and forger of weapons who also happened to shoe horses – invariably war horses or chariot horses, because he was frequently seconded to the army. The farrier, on the other hand, although he also shod horses, had a rather more elevated status as a kind of horse doctor, and could be asked for advice on the buying and selling of horses. That, at least, was their historical distinction.

The farrier's craft dates back to the Germanic and Celtic peoples, both of whom were knowledgeable in it long before the Romans came to Rye. The Normans – themselves of course originally a Norse people – used farriers in a similar sense, and when they invaded England in 1066 they brought their horses by the thousand, and their farriers with them.

In about 1356, the farriers formed themselves into a Guild or Fellowship of Farriers, duly mentioned in the Records of the City of London, to oversee and govern their craft, to ensure high standards and prevent shoddy workmanship. There were rules and penalties for poor work, and a farrier found guilty of bad workmanship was fined. For a second offence he was made 'to forswear the same trade within the city for ever'. Fellows, if asked for advice on buying a horse, were not encouraged to ask for 'gifts', thus ensuring them a reputation for professionalism and impartiality, and neither could they undertake treatment of a horse unless they were reasonably certain of success, on pain of being struck off.

In 1590, they were granted a coat of arms ascribed by the College of Heralds with the motto 'Vi et Virtute': 'By Strength and Virtue'. Sadly, most of their records were destroyed in the Great Fire of 1666, and the next we know of them is that they were granted a Royal Charter by Charles II in 1674.

By the mid-nineteenth century the Company of Farriers had begun to lose some of its reputation, and in order to repair the damage and re-establish its credentials, a Registration Scheme for Shoeing Smiths was inaugurated. Under this scheme a Registration Committee would compile a register of all farriers, listed by county, and hold examinations to determine the proficiency of their members. These tests are still conducted today, and are accepted by the trade as the standard of competency for which they were intended.

In 1973, the ILPH, whose scheme had until then operated independently, decided instead to pay a grant to the Worshipful Company of Farriers, so that in future ILPH-sponsored farriers would be qualified under the aegis of the industry's own body. And, just as happened with the Royal School of Veterinary Studies, the two organizations have continued to support one another ever since.

In spite of all this activity, however, towards the end of the 1970s things began to go awry for the ILPH. It was a time of contrasts. On the one hand, between the years of 1972 and 1974 the ILPH became, financially, worth its first million. Careful management of income since before the war, under the watchful eye of Anne Colvin, had contributed to steady and sensible growth (thanks in no small part to the advice of Norman McLeod of Scrimgeours, who, incidentally, was to play an even more influential part in the more recent history of the ILPH). On the other hand, the vastly increased activities and the number of new projects, particularly overseas, meant that the running costs of the charity had risen steeply. In spite of its apparent affluence, there was a point at which costs had accelerated so sharply that expenditure came close to outstripping income.

It was not that there was any lack of motivation, and yet at the same time it seemed, for a brief while at least, as if the ILPH had somehow lost its way. Perhaps it was a reflection of the malaise that seemed to affect many aspects of both the political and social climate of the seventies.

It was a decade that opened with all the controversy and suspicion caused by Britain's entry into the Common Market – would we lose our identity, our autonomy, and become a colony of Europe? Or was this the way forward? – and it closed with all the disaffection that gave rise to punk and anarchy in the UK, to the National Front and anti-racism riots.

The ILPH had become to an extent a divided organization. It was divided physically between Norfolk and London: Overa, where Captain Bennington, the Director – the executive – was based, and Camden Town, where the Head Office then was, where Anne Colvin, the Secretary, ran the legislating arm. And gradually, the split began to manifest itself in other ways. Charities such as the ILPH attract people of passion and conviction. This is the motive force that drives them. The potent belief that what they do is unchallengeably right, not only a moral obligation but a necessity, is what makes charities successful. If a commercial enterprise were to be staffed by a team with as much enthusiasm, as much determination to see the end result achieved – and achieved without compromise – that enterprise too would become a success in pretty short order.

However, what is not always to the benefit of the organization – commercial or charitable – is when two equally passionate natures pull in opposite directions. What affected the ILPH was not so much a division of outlook as a clash of personalities. Anne Colvin and Charles Bennington met sometimes, head on.

Anne Colvin knew every thread and thought of the organization. She knew the running of it, what it was doing from day to day. She had known Ada Cole, she had organized the early meetings which had given the League its life. She knew and remembered every bitter fight it took to get that first Act on the statute book. She even knew all the members' names.

The coins she had collected on Flag Days and the funds she had invested when the charity was in its infancy, she had personally handled. She had the workings of the whole effort in the palm of her hand and had eaten, breathed and slept the ILPH every day, non-stop, since 1925.

Charles Bennington knew it because he was out there, with the horses. He saw them on the trains and in the trucks and in the rusty holds of cargo vessels that docked in Italy. He saw them slaughtered in their thousands, and he helped to save them in their thousands.

The Council meetings of the day must have been interesting.

And it was not in fact until the late 1980s that the good sense and perspicacity of Norman McLeod resolved the conflicts within the ILPH and took it forward into a new future.

I arranged to meet Charles Bennington at three o'clock on Thursday, 16 January 1992. I spoke to him on the telephone at eleven o'clock that morning.

He died at one o'clock that afternoon.

I was sorry never to have met him. I know I would have liked him. I like old-fashioned horsemen who call a spade a spade.

His ashes were scattered over Overa Farm a few months later.

Whenever I go there, I think of what he did. And I think of him because his spirit lives in every board and nail and box and tree and shrub in that place; it lives in every horse that crosses its threshold, and every handful of feed that is placed in front of them. It lives in every groom who runs a dandy-brush across every horse's back and in every hand that is raised to protect or cure or school any horse that finds itself grazing in those fields, beside the river, at Overa, his home.

SEVEN

I t is all too easy to forget that the story of any organization like the ILPH consists of more than founders and secretaries, chairmen and directors.

The ILPH would not exist today without the many others who have served its cause in any one of a dozen different capacities in its formative years. Some of these have been men and women of rare distinction or unusual character, and one such, who was in a sense the first forerunner of the field officers of today, was Mona Huskie.

The role of the investigator in the ILPH was Ada Cole's idea. Investigation uncovered abuses and provided the raw material from which they compiled the evidence and the statistics they needed in order to bring about change. From the earliest days, Ada Cole wished 'to engage someone with initiative, energy and accuracy, to investigate and report . . .' Enter Mona Huskie.

Like Ada, she was a diminutive woman – as indeed was Anne Colvin (then Sadie Baum) – and on first encounter they must have seemed an eccentric trio, running their eccentric organization bang in the middle of the Great Depression, working on behalf of old horses while men and women were begging in the streets.

Like Ada Cole, Mona Huskie believed passionately in her work. But unlike both Ada Cole and Anne Colvin, she was hot-headed; she was never averse to giving a dealer a black eye and was reputed to have lambasted more than a few with her handbag. She appears throughout the early literature of the ILPH, where she seems to have been regarded as a bit of a loose cannon. Incensed by indifference, she had a habit of lashing out on the spot, either with that bag of hers or with well-aimed and potent invective – a habit which not surprisingly got her into trouble. Understandable her reactions may have been, but she could not seem to appreciate that in the long run, calm and objective reporting will gain ten times the ground won by punching the guilty on the nose.

Independent by nature and fiery by temperament, she could not be employed for long. Nevertheless, her early days with the ILPH bore fruit, because – always the champion of the cause of ponies, which had been erroneously left out of the provisions of the 1937 Exportation of Horses Act – she went on to found the Horse and Pony Protection Association, commonly known as HAPPA. HAPPA does a marvellous job today with both horses and ponies all over the country. There is close and friendly co-operation between its representatives and those of the ILPH, and at any horse sale you might find groups of HAPPA and ILPH field officers monitoring the proceedings together, swapping notes.

On the ground, at grass-roots level, there is no room for squabbles between charities whose aims are similar – especially not when the welfare of the animals whose protection is their object is at stake.

Another formidable activist in the tradition of Mona Huskie was Anne Newton, who ran the Leeds branch of the ILPH in the 1950s. The *Illustrated Magazine* of 8 November 1952, in an article headed 'She Buys Life for Horses', describes her tactics thus:

The auctioneer's hammer was raised to knock another of Britain's fine Shire horses down to a horsemeat buyer. 'Stop the sale!' cried a cultured voice in the gloomy Manchester auction yard, noisy with the cracking of whips. Mrs Anne Newton pushed her way to the front with a bundle of pound notes in her hand. Dealers and hangers-on turned quickly. The auctioneer poised his hammer in mid-air. And a few moments later Mrs Newton, blonde and measuring six feet from her French heels to the top of her feathered hat, was leading away Dick, a dark bay horse who had worked for the railways in Leeds for more than ten years. She has paid fifty guineas for him. Dick, the first of the Leeds railway horses to become redundant because of mechanisation, was being rescued by Mrs Newton after an urgent appeal from his driver, who did not want to see him slaughtered. Since that day she has bought twenty railway horses from Leeds, Manchester, Liverpool, Hull and Skipton, eighteen ponies – including five pit ponies – and eighteen donkeys ... Some she has bought after a dramatic last-minute rush to the doors of the slaughterhouse; some she had bought after they were led off the boats from Ireland . . . Crank or crusader? Whichever she is, Mrs Newton gets results.

Mrs Newton once ran a fashion house in Leeds before she became involved with the ILPH, but she would have had to have gone some way to match the style and panache of Olivia Steuart-Menzies, who ran the Newbury branch of the ILPH in the fifties. Mrs Steuart-Menzies' enthusiasm – apart from horses – was for cars. The first woman to race at Brooklands, she worked for a time for Malcolm Campbell, and bought his first Bluebird. In a 1924 Mercedes-Benz she took part in hill-climbs in Monte Carlo, where she won prizes; one, her daughter Jean McDougall recalls, 'just for being a woman'. She owned the Black Cat garage in Wigmore Street and would herself dress up in a chauffeur's uniform and hire out her expensive limousines. An accomplished horsewoman, after the war she took in injured racehorses, discovering that she had a special knack of curing them. Several who had been in her hands went on, says Jean McDougall, 'to win a lovely lot of races'.

Dudley Alexander, yet another character of the fifties, also shared his love of horses with the love of another mode of transport – this time trains. He had a light model railway which, for the technically minded, was a ten-and-a-half-inch gauge on which ran a 4-6-4 steam locomotive with a working pressure of seventy pounds per square inch. This little train had been used during the war to demonstrate the vulnerability of rolling stock to fighter pilots attacking enemy freight and armoured trains. Afterwards its use was devoted to the ILPH, and with it Alexander created valuable publicity and raised substantial funds.

Most unusual – not to say eccentric – of all was Dorothy Lawrence of the Bedford branch. Miss Lawrence owned a large grey Shire named Dobbyn, of whom she used to tell this story: one day, Dobbyn, who lived on water meadows beside a river, heard a child cry out, and duly ambled over to the river, where he beheld the urchin, drowning, in midstream. Slithering down the bank, the huge horse waded out into the foaming waters, plucked the child from the torrent in his teeth and bore it safely to the bank, where he was found by the happy parents, licking its tear-stained face.

THE SHADOW BEHIND THE HORSE

AN APPEAL TO BRITISH FAIR PLAY

Do you know that British horses are still being exported to the Continent to be slaughtered for food, but that in many cases they are bought by dealers in the open market for further work and suffer a fate worse than death, eking out a pitiable existence —ill-fed and cruelly treated—till death comes at last as a merciful release in some foreign slaughter-house ?

THE SHADOW BEHIND THE HORSE

How would YOU feel if such a fate were to befall one of your horses ? And what do you suppose a foreigner thinks of us who boast of our good sportsmanship and sell our old horses into slavery abroad ?

Will you not help to end this terrible reproach ?

Send your donation or write for particulars to :—

THE INTERNATIONAL LEAGUE TO PREVENT THE EXPORT OF HORSES FOR BUTCHERY

(International League for Horses),

4, BLOOMSBURY SQUARE,
LONDON, W.C.1

It was posters and leaflets like this that the young distributed in the 1930s

Ada Cole, founder of the ILPH, shows the determination which enabled her to succeed in the face of all opposition

Brigadier General Sir George Cockerill, Honorary Director of the ILPH from 1931 until his death in 1957 at the age of ninety

Sketch by Brian de Grimeau of English horses in a Brussels meat market

THE TRAFFIC IN IRISH HORSES

FROM GALWAY TO PARIS

A 700-Mile Journey to Slaughter

[*Many people have been disturbed by the growing traffic in live horses and donkeys for slaughter on the Continent, and sometimes in this country. Animal slaughter is not pleasant to contemplate, but a meat-eating community must not be sentimental about it. There is evidence, however, that the Irish traffic, now between twenty thousand and thirty-five thousand horses a year, is accompanied by needless cruelty and avoidable suffering. A strong movement of protest has arisen in Eire, but the Government has refused to check the traffic.*

In this and succeeding articles a member of the staff of the "Manchester Guardian" gives the results of his investigations in Ireland and France.]

PARIS, JUNE.

At 10 43 on a sunny morning here a few days ago the crumpled form of a little black Irish mare twitched in the swelling pool of her own blood on an abattoir floor. Then, abruptly, there was a final shudder and she lay still. For Minstrel Girl it was the end of the trail, an agonising trail that had begun in County Galway five days and 700 miles ago. Or was it quite the end? They had said that the captive-bolt killer was almost instantaneous, but her eyes were still bright and wide open as a lanky French butcher in a spattered smock that had once been white reached for the long knife that swung from his belt. There was the bright flash of steel in the sunlight; then a sudden cascade of rich crimson spouting from the jagged slash in the little mare's throat.

The laconic Frenchman in Stall 16 went swiftly about his business. He reached for a flat, circular pan and flicked it into place, catching the cataract from the horse's jugular vein. It filled in less than a minute. As he transferred the crimson contents to a waiting wooden churn he used the toe of his clog to nudge a second pan into place on the slippery concrete floor. That was the moment when Minstrel Girl made her final, shuddering movement. Her forelegs stiffened and trembled; for an instant her head lifted into the air, and then it was down and twitching in the brimming pan of her own blood. And then suddenly it stopped moving; one eye sank from view into the liquid; the other gazed skyward sightless as it clouded over gradually.

THE LAST DAYS

It is the reporter's job to write about what he sees as factually and with as little emotion as possible, and

3

Extract from an article by Patrick Keatley which appeared in the *Manchester Guardian* in June 1952. His series of articles exposing the trade in live horses helped publicize the cause

The farrier's farewell: this man's three cherished horses were taken in by Cherry Tree Farm after he wrote to the Queen Mother about his fears for their future

Redundant workers: vanners and cobs like these lined up on Dublin's North Wall were exported live for slaughter right up until the mid-1960s

Roger Macchia indicates the kind of unprotected metal that can cause horrific injuries to horses at sea. This sharp edge – just about at head height for a horse – is actually in the doorway of a horse pen on this ship

Dudley Alexander's light railway at Brockenhurst, Hants., raised funds for the ILPH in the fifties and early sixties

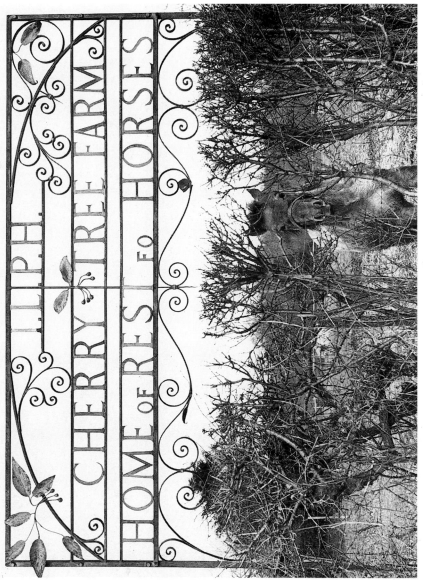

Tuppence, an early resident, greets visitors to Cherry Tree beneath the farm's
specially designed wrought-iron sign

Dartmoor ponies wild on the moor. The ILPH has worked hard to ensure that
Britain's native ponies are not sold abroad for meat

It is certainly true that Dobbyn did sterling work on behalf of the ILPH, opening fêtes and gymkhanas at which he would auction goods by holding them in his mouth and waving them around – so perhaps his story is not so unlikely after all.

Ronald Burchnell joined the ILPH in 1930 and remained a stalwart of the League until his retirement in 1965. As a boy he had worked in his father's saddlery business: horses were in his blood. During the war he served as a member of Bomber Command, returning to the ILPH when it was over as Chief Investigator for England and Overseas.

In the sixties, Burchnell worked closely with Charles Benn-ington, and it was undoubtedly the work they did together which laid down the framework for the present-day field-officer system which Bennington was to mastermind. Bennington was later to comment on the dedication and selflessness with which Burchnell carried out his duties no matter what the difficulties he might encounter. When the ILPH was short of funds he would hitch-hike across the Channel in order to reach the horses on which he was required to report.

Back in Britain he was no less tireless. He kept statistics on slaughterhouses – the only nationally co-ordinated and collated statistics available at that time. His figures make interesting reading: by 1959, for instance, the number of slaughterhouses licensed to produce horsemeat for human consumption had fallen from sixty to twenty-three. Many knackers' yards had been shut down – some as a direct result of ILPH pressure – for inhumane practices, and the number of horses slaughtered dropped in the same period from 52,899 in 1952 to 12,908 in 1959.

Burchnell visited auctions and farm sales and wherever possible recorded the numbers and condition of horses sold for slaughter. He attended sales of Exmoor and Dartmoor ponies – a good deal of work was done by the ILPH to improve their conditions and prevent their sale for slaughter, as it was with the ponies of the New Forest – and the dispersal sales of railway horses and pit ponies.

But for all his devotion there was more to his life than horses: he was a talented pianist, and had played in orchestras conducted by Malcolm Sargent. When he died in 1974, Charles Bennington went to his funeral at Bourne Abbey and was astonished to find the abbey packed with mourners and the service taken by the Dean. He had not realized – though he was no doubt deeply gratified to discover – the esteem in which Ronald Burchnell had been held in his home town.

Tom Banks was the first of many to join the ILPH from the ranks of the cavalry or the mounted police – yet another inspiration of Charles Bennington's, and a tradition which still serves the ILPH well today. A Scot from Musselburgh, he had enlisted at the age of seventeen and spent seven years with the 7th Hussars before twenty-six years with the Leeds City Police. Within a month of his retirement Bennington had persuaded him to join the ILPH as its northern representative – a post he held for sixteen years – prompting Austen Haywood, then Assistant Chief Constable, to remark that never had a retiring policeman transferred to another job so neatly or so suitably.

Tom Banks did not confine his work to the north of England – like Ronald Burchnell, he travelled to sales and markets as far afield as Aberdeen and Hampshire – but by 1978 he had, in the words of the *Yorkshire Evening Post*, 'deflected retired police horses and others from all over the north into the League's rest homes'. Adel was the first police horse to end his days in peace at Cherry Tree Farm thanks to Tom Banks: he was twenty-three when he retired and had reached the ripe old age of thirty-two when he had to be put down. One of Banks's biggest jobs was finding homes for the pit ponies which were being laid off in large numbers – he reported that he had re-homed between fifty and sixty of them in one year alone.

Charles Wilgose, Tom Banks's successor, conducted a survey of pit ponies for the ILPH and found that in general, contrary to popular supposition, the conditions under which they worked were good. At the end of the seventies there were 210 ponies still at work in Britain's mines, seventy-eight of them at one pit – Madderley – alone. But regulations ensured that the ponies worked the same hours and the same shifts as the men and after each shift they were brought above ground for stabling. None was stabled underground, and each was given one day's rest per week. The pit ponies that went to Cherry Tree into the care of Ian Gibbs had been generally well kept, and, according to the records at least, their most regular visitors were the miners who had looked after them and worked alongside them. And there was never any truth to the old tale that pit ponies go blind.

There were equine characters, too, who did their share of work for the ILPH, largely as ambassadors to the public. In the same year that Charlie Wilgose joined from the Sheffield Mounted Police – 1978 – a four-legged colleague from the South Yorkshire force arrived alongside him. Brigadier had lost an eye during a riot at a football match when an agitator had tossed a brick at him (horses nowadays wear protective eyeshields). The old horse, a big grey of great presence and superb conformation, became the personal mount of Charles Bennington and under him led many an Open Day Parade and many a sponsored ride. At the Sheffield Horse Show, with his former rider Police Officer Neil Blades, he received a standing ovation, and during his years with the ILPH was the recipient of sackfuls of Christmas cards and poems sent by his many fans.

And no story of the ILPH would be complete without mention of Copenhagen, the gallant horse of the Blues and Royals who, like Sefton, was severely injured in the IRA bomb in Hyde Park in 1982. The ILPH has given Copenhagen an honourable retirement and a home for life. But there is no doubt that he and horses like him repay the ILPH a hundredfold in terms of the publicity and promotional opportunities that their presence engenders.

In any organization the work done behind desks and in the office is no less vital than the work of those who are, so to speak, in the front line, and the ILPH is no exception. The ILPH was for many years steered by the cool head and able administration of Stella Baum.

Stella told me that secretly she had always harboured a special interest in engineering, arising from the war when, like a number of women, she had had to learn what had until then been a man's job – welding – when the men were called up on active service. Afterwards, although she had worked in machine-tool factories and for BOC, and had studied at Hendon Technical College, she was never able to pursue her hidden goal. How many women of her generation found and then lost their true vocation as a result of the war we can only guess. But the ILPH has every reason to be grateful to Stella Baum.

Married to Anne Colvin's brother John, Stella, like many family members, initially found herself roped in to help out with ILPH business when they were short-staffed or under unusual pressure in the office. However, administrative skills soon made her contribution invaluable, and in 1972 she began work for the ILPH on a formal basis. It was she who took on the burden of the office work and the correspondence, and she who helped Anne Colvin reorganize her complex and sometimes archaic card-index systems. And it was she who kept the day-to-day business of the charity on an even keel throughout occasionally troubled times.

And all over the country there were branches and individual members whose names may be unrecorded but without whose sup-port ILPH could never have continued its work. The enthusiasts who gave their time and energy to bring-and-buy-sales, jumble sales, coffee mornings, dog shows and gymkhanas. The ILPH archives record concerts where only horsey music was played, carol services, special horsemen's services which drew large crowds – or should I say congregations? There were treasure hunts and swimming competitions and poetry recitals and everything else besides. There were Flag Days when the Cavalry Club gave the ILPH a free stand on its ground, and there was even a Horses' Christmas Fund which gave the money it raised to the buying of blankets and fodder for needy horses and donkeys and an extra feed for those lucky enough to be around at the time. Finally, there was a Housewife's Dream Competition which provided the winner with whatever her dream was, which invariably turned out to be a home for some old work-worn horse with an eye to an easy life.

Of course, these are the kinds of events that are common to any charity. But nevertheless, the ILPH does not forget that it is on the generosity of such people and the schemes they dream up to raise money that it depends.

PART FOUR

Hands Across the Sea: The ILPH Abroad

EIGHT

'When is St Stephen's Day?' Tony Schormann asked.

I shook my head. No idea.

'The day before the races in Ting Maling Malu.' He chuckled and winked and poured another whisky.

'Before I raced I worked for a firm that folded,' he added casually, talking about his background. 'I'm not surprised it folded,' he said, settling into an armchair. 'To be sure, someone was taking money out of the till for a weekend's fishing.'

Tony's got what you might call a bit of the blarney in him – that or a chip of it in his pocket.

His background is horses: he trained as a lad in Captain Harty's yard in Chapelizard as a professional jockey, and while still young was advised to ride as an amateur in England for a while, which he did with some success in point-to-pointing. He has sheaves of newspaper cuttings and plenty of photographs. 'Ah, it's better than show-jumping,' he went on, scratching his chin. 'It's all over in five minutes and you've either won or lost or you're on the floor or on a stretcher; but anyway it's over and if you're still in one piece you can go home.'

Lying in a bed in hospital once, with most of the bones in his body broken, he was visited by Group Captain Rupert Nash, Director of ILPH Eire at the time, who looked down on the bandaged figure and sighed, 'Oh, Tony, I'm afraid you were born to hang!'

Tony tells the story against himself, as only a man confident of his own abilities and fibre can. He's full of stories, good ones. He told one about a horse seen walking on its joints: he went off to find it only to discover it belonged to a terrorist who was wanted for murder.

'I was warned not to go near him,' Tony said, 'because he had taken drink and was sure to pull a gun on me, but you know how it is ... I don't scare that easy ...'

He got the horse.

He's full of the most Irish of expressions. He told me about a fellow in town who had given up his former ways, pulled himself together and now had 'a bit of standing in the community instead of a bit of squatting'. And how a certain horse he knew 'couldn't run fast enough to keep herself warm'; how the same horse eventually fell and 'ain't that a sure sign that she couldn't move her legs quick enough to keep out of her own way?' Of a 'sly divil of a country bastard' we met who talked and talked, and after a minute or two of listening, looking around him, Tony said, 'I can hear the bees, but I can't see the honey.' And how the same man 'wasn't worth the powder that would shoot him'.

But it was a particular expression of Tony's that made the hair prickle on the back of my neck, because it's an expression only a horseman would use, and he meant it. When he was angered by something he knew was wrong, you would hear him 'calling all the Horse Ghosts' to put it right.

Tony has pale penetrating eyes, is a horseman's horseman and is the ILPH Field Director for Eire. He lives just in front of a farm called Stepaside, set high in the hills behind Dun Laoghaire, above Dublin, on a yellow-gorsed piece of ground on the side of Three Rock Mountain. Stretched out below the farm the land falls away down to the old Leopardstown racecourse, 'this side of McGrath's gallops: one, one-and-a-half, and two-mile peat gallops, straight five furlongs: terrific gallops – now going under a housing estate. A pity. A great pity.' He pointed down to a stand of trees adjacent to the gallops. 'Orby,' he said, 'winner of the English Derby in the early part of the century is buried in the trees down there. A great horse. Best in all Ireland. Went over there and beat all them Protestant horses!'

We had a couple of drinks and then walked over Stepaside Farm. 'The ILPH bought this old place in 1960 for twelve thousand pounds. Of course it was just a piece of rough ground then, but it was dear enough, to be sure. But they needed a farm for all the problems with the export trade, and a mighty fine battle that turned out to be.'

Stepaside Farm was home to hundreds of horses bound for slaughter, as well as tinkers' horses bought in appalling condition, horses that Tony put right and found homes for; and ponies, don-keys, ex-racehorses, vanners, heavy horses – the lot.

Stepaside itself was sold by the ILPH in 1991, but Tony is still there, carrying on the work which was begun by Eleanor Whitton, the first ILPH representative in Eire, back in 1928. When she died, her daughter Constance took up the cudgels, and after her came Group Captain Rupert Nash, CBE, and after him Tony.

In all the history of the ILPH, Ireland's is the most telling, because it was and still is in some sense an enigma. At one extreme there are the tinkers' ponies, which are often found in the most terrible condition. Lady Talbot de Malahide, who worked on behalf of the ILPH in the 1940s, once stopped one on the road because it was lame and found that the frogs of its feet had completely rotted away. Yet at the other extreme, Thoroughbreds sell for millions through the sale rings at Goffs, where the Sangsters, the Maktoums, the Aga Khan and the other great names of the racing world flock to buy them; and the studs of Kildare and Tipperary are among the richest in the world.

From Ireland come some of the world's greatest horses, and yet Ireland continued to export horses under the most appalling condi-tions long after the Exportation of Horses Act had put an end to their suffering in Great Britain.

Tony talks about the North Wall in Dublin, where the old horses would line up for export. 'It was real out-of-sight, out-of-mind stuff,' he explained. 'Of course there were rules, you know, vets and things, but you line up a couple of hundred mixed horses in the howling wind and lashing rain at night and how much chance has a vet got?'

There are Minimum Values in Ireland now, but the present mood of the EC is to remove them and return to a live trade, because those are the rules of the majority of countries within the Community. That men and women in power can even think like this – that countries which currently regulate against the export of live horses for slaughter should be at risk of losing those regulations – exhibits a monstrous flaw in the whole system of Euro-legislation. What we need is a ban on live exports for slaughter altogether, for all livestock, all animals.

But in the Irish Dáil this is an old chestnut.

It was the subject of a lively parliamentary debate in November 1953, when proposals to prohibit the export of live horses and substitute a dressed meat trade in its place were heatedly discussed. It is worth quoting some of the arguments in full here, both for and against, because they encapsulate, with typically Irish eloquence, not only the situation in Eire at the time but also the issues that have been central to the ILPH throughout its history.

Among the arguments against was that the farmers of Ireland needed the money they received from the sale of live horses in order to survive. Moreover, cruelty was a matter of course where meat production was concerned. It was a fact of life; it could not be helped, and would be found in the slaughter of any livestock. Mr Walsh, Minister of Agriculture, went on to suggest that in his opinion, a horse was of no greater value than a cow. He was reminded that he himself had lately paid £250,000 for a single horse, to which he replied that the horse he had bought for that princely sum had not been destined for slaughter. 'We bought him,' said the Minister, 'for the purpose of making money out of him and for the purpose of enhancing the reputation of our bloodstock.'

Dr ffrench O'Carroll, in support of the proposals, gave the Minister short shrift:

'The Minister has made some amazing statements. He said that you could not stop the export of one type of horse. There is no foundation for that. It was stopped without the slightest difficulty in England. It is the Exportation of Horses Act 1937. They just laid down that horses over a certain age and under a certain value should not be exported. It was as simple as that.

'The Minister suggests that where there is blood there is cruelty. What he meant is beyond my comprehension ... The suggestion that the death rate on the ship journey (for horses in transit) is low, and that therefore there is no cruelty is quite fallacious. You cannot assume that just because the death rate is low there is no cruelty.'

He produced records:

Dieppe, December 18, 1951.

PRESTER LILY (Lot 113 and Shipping No. 119) – 15-year-old mare by Prester John, covered by Erno, last service July 7th. Winner on the flat and over hurdles, bred by Mr J. H. Peard: registered vol.

XXXI G.S.B. Sold by Mr P. J. Fleming at Goffs' November Sales, 1951 for 20 guineas. Traced to Vaugirard Slaughterhouse, Paris.

Dieppe, December 18, 1951

OATMEAL (Lot 101) – 12-year-old Cameronian mare covered by Arco. This mare was a winner in England and placed eight times: dam of Suemick (2-year-old winner in England). This mare left behind a yearling by Niccolo Dell'Arca and a colt foal by Naucide. Bred by Mr A. F. Bassell: registered vol. XXXI G.S.B. Sold through Goffs' November Sales for 25 guineas. Traced to Vaugirard Slaughterhouse, Paris.

Dieppe, December 18, 1951.

MINISTER ACRES (Lot 610 and Shipping No. 108) – 2-year-old Tudor Minstrel colt, the property of Sir Percy Lorraine. Half-brother to Queenpot, winner of over £17,000, including the One Thousand Guineas. This colt was in training up to the time of the sales and sold for 22 guineas at Goffs. Traced to Vaugirard Slaughterhouse, Paris.

There were thousands more, enhancing the reputation of Irish blood-stock, or, as Dr ffrench O'Carroll argues with bitter irony, enhancing the reputation of Ireland.

Even a Belgian constable, one Monsieur Lerno, who witnessed the terrible state of horses as they were unloaded at Antwerp, thought it was his duty to expose this state of affairs in a letter addressed to the Belgian SPCA. He wrote:

The horses are completely exhausted. There were 166 on board, coming from Ireland. The tired and seriously injured horses can hardly stand up. 75% are injured at the hindquarters. Tail hair has been torn out and the tails are covered with blood. During the voyage four horses died of exhaustion and were thrown overboard. The inhuman manner of transporting these animals shows that too many horses are piled into too small and badly equipped ships. Two customs officials who were with me agreed that it was already high time to put an end to this method of transportation. The fact that these horses are intended for slaughter is no reason to treat them badly . . .'

But the words of Mr Larkin were perhaps the most powerful of all. 'In my opinion,' he said,

> there is just as much, or probably more, cruelty inflicted on those other animals (cattle and pigs) in our own country than on horses outside the country. I do not think we should take particular pride in that . . . it seems to me that the one argument that is not defensible is that if there was a case proved in regard to the export of horses we should not interfere with it because it would represent an economic loss to our people. That is an argument I cannot accept. It is the same type of argument we have had to contend with in regard to many other features of our national life. We have had it in regard not only to animals but to human beings. We could not help the people in the slums because of the proprietorial rights of the owners. We could not interfere with child labour in factories because we would interfere with the rights of the owners who exploit them. It is also suggested now that we cannot interfere with any trade in livestock, whether horses, sheep or pigs, because we may interfere with the economic interests of those who bred those animals.

In the end, however, not all the skill and reason with which they argued could win the day, and the proposal to ban the export of live horses for slaughter was defeated, by fifty-two votes to twenty-six.

It took two disasters at sea, with all their attendant adverse publicity, and twelve more years of dedicated work by ILPH representatives Constance Whitton and Rupert Nash, before the trade was finally brought to an end.

On 29 December 1959, the bodies of twelve horses were washed up on the beaches of South Wales. They came from a consignment of a hundred horses shipped from Dublin aboard the SS *City of Waterford*, bound for Dieppe. The ship ran into heavy seas, and the horses that were killed, thrown about in the hold by the force of the storm, were winched out and dumped overboard. In Dublin, Mr Crowe, ILPH agent, had counted 142 horses on board the ship, and in Dieppe he counted 95 get off, eleven of which had to be shot on the docks, so badly were they damaged. It was elementary mathematics to deduce that 47 had died at sea.

The ILPH, in conjunction with the Irish SPCA, urged the government to investigate, and the case was taken up by the *Irish Times*. Vested interests fought hard. A press release issued in reply read: 'The farmers, dealers and shippers of this country greatly resent the suppression of ... the horse trade by those who are waging a one-sided, misinformed campaign against it in the press ...' An editorial in the *Farmer's Gazette* followed, headed 'Horse Sense or Hysterics': '... horse breeders and buyers, racing interests, seamen, shippers and dockers as well as farmers are being pilloried just because, as a matter of chance, a violent storm blew up after a sea captain had sailed with a cargo of live horses in calm conditions.' But it was too late. This time the tide had begun to turn against them. The government – which, to give it its due, had declared as early as 1957 that it was prepared to consider the slaughter of horses on Irish soil and the export of carcasses instead of meat 'on the hoof' – bowed to the sudden increase of pressure that the *City of Waterford* incident had provoked. In 1961, regulations were introduced to prohibit the export of horses over seven years of age, and in March 1963 this limit was reduced to five years, except for horses certified fit for work. A model slaughterhouse, 'ready and capable to deal with the entire Irish trade and successfully export chilled meat to the Continent', was established by A. M. McNeill at Straffan, Kildare. The dealers cold-shouldered it, but the ILPH and the Dublin SPCA – both bulk buyers of old, cast horses – did not.

Still the new laws had loopholes. In 1964, the SS *City of Cork* left for the Continent with a cargo of horses for slaughter – even though they were fit for work. When a storm similar to the one the *City of Waterford* had encountered met with similar results, there was a second, similar public outcry. The government could not afford any further embarrassment, and on 7 March 1964, Charles Haughey, then Minister of Agriculture, placed a ban on the export for slaughter of all live horses, of all ages.

Today, except for the odd rumours of horses, ponies or donkeys being smuggled across the sea, the trade has to all intents and purposes been stopped. But even now the ILPH cannot relax its vigilance lest, as is the danger in England, pressures from within the European Community result in its reintroduction.

*

Back in the 1940s, Sir Frederick Hobday, chief veterinary adviser to the ILPH, summed up the situation in Ireland thus: 'The League has certainly struck its axe at the root of a very big tree, for Southern Ireland is the most curious anomaly of cruelty and kindness where its horses are concerned . . .'

When I went over in 1992, Tony Schormann took me through the whole gamut. We visited the notorious Smithfield market, where scenes of callousness are still common. 'But it's no good screaming and raving and swearing at some silly eedyot who can't tell a horse from a whore,' said Tony. 'You want to be a bit crafty: win him round, because you'll never beat him round, you know.'

We visited the stately stud at Kildagan, where Sheik Mohammed's stallions live in ashlar-stone houses grander than the grand houses of the barons of Berkshire. We toured their manicured paddocks, walked their manicured gallops, visited the air-conditioned foaling boxes and gazed into the high-tech machines that maintain a constant temperature and 'wipe the foals' bottoms for them'.

We went to Finglas, where the street urchins keep their ponies on scratches of grass outside high-rise flats. Tony told me of a man who saw one of these kids take a pony into the flats, and caught him just as he was leading the pony into the lift. 'You're not taking that pony up in that, are you?' he said. 'Sure,' the lad replied, 'the stairs would finish him.'

And if I had to choose where I would sooner spend the day, at Kildagan Stud or Finglas, it would be Finglas every time. Finglas, with these kids and their ponies, belting round bareback, enjoying the thrill only a pony can give you when you're ten; enjoying the heady feeling of making that first big jump, the one you thought you never could, then doing it again and again and thinking a lot of that pony for giving you the guts to try.

Finglas was a little piece of Ireland that felt really Irish to me, though I suppose it was just a bally great dump all filled with high-rise blocks. But it had heart and you could feel it, hear its strong Irish voices and read its character, far richer than all the smooth paddocks and grand houses and glossy Thoroughbreds I would care to look upon. I thought it was wonderful, Ireland wonderful.

I left Tony worrying about his old mare: she was due to foal, and was a couple of weeks overdue. She was a one-eyed Reilly, to be sure. A couple of days later, I was at my home on the Welsh borders when he telephoned. His mare had foaled. A filly foal. And I drank a toast to her, to Tony, his wife and family, and to all the horse ghosts.

NINE

The first steps of the ILPH into a truly international arena came as early as the 1930s, when Sir George Cockerill drafted an International Convention in order to secure a measure of protection for horses being transported long distances by sea. This draft he presented to the League of Nations with recommendations for discussion. It was the first time that any request for the consideration of animal welfare had been put before that august assembly.

The ILPH had been prompted to take this action by three transatlantic shipments of horses which arrived in Europe in 1930 and 1931. The SS *Van Belge*, from Buenos Aires, had docked in Le Havre on 24 March 1930 after a journey of thirty-three days at sea. The horses on board were in a deplorable condition. The following year the SS *Macedonier* arrived in Antwerp after thirty-six days at sea, with twenty-two live horses, all that were left of the original cargo of sixty. And on 24 July a steamship docked at Le Havre with a cargo of 150 horses from Halifax, Canada.

All these shipments had been condemned by La Ligue Française pour la Protection du Cheval and La Société Protection des Animaux, and the ILPH, which until then had concentrated its efforts exclusively on the trade in English horses, but felt impelled to add its support to the objectors.

Sir George was never slow to take his protests to the most effective authority, and in 1935 his International Convention, as it became, was adopted by the League of Nations. It laid down that 'exporting countries must take steps to see that the animals are properly loaded and suitably fed and that they receive all necessary attention in order to avoid all unnecessary suffering'. A protocol attached to the Convention emphasized the need for attendants on long journeys, and for animals to travel by the shortest routes and as far as practicable by accelerated goods trains. By 1937, more than a dozen countries had ratified it. America and Canada were signatories, and though Argentina at the time was not, shipments from South America, for the time being at least, stopped. This was an important step: it was considered to be the first towards the eventual establishment of an International Charter for the Protection of Animals – and it came from the ILPH.

So far so good. But the ILPH could not afford to relax its vigilance for a moment. The Second World War, as it did in so many areas, changed things, and after it was over shipments began again, as barbaric as before. In May 1947, a shipment of horses sailed from North America to Poland via Denmark. Of a cargo of 720, 200 died at sea, and a further 58 in port, at Copenhagen. A few days later another shipment arrived, this time of a staggering 1503 horses, of which 305 were dead. The ships had been equipped for cattle only, and many horses had been loaded on to the top deck where they received the brunt of the Atlantic weather – gales and high seas, driving rain and ice, followed by scorching sunlight. Animals in the holds had choked through lack of ventilation.

It seems extraordinary that anyone could have been callous enough to load horses like this, or ignorant enough to suppose they would survive. The only possible conclusion is quite simply that they did not care. Sir George, however, as before, took his protest to the top: to the United States Ambassador in London. And for the second time, the shipments stopped.

Now, however, other issues overseas began to attract the ILPH's attention. A trade in horses from Malta to Tunis had begun, which they took steps to regulate. In Australia they took issue with the poisoning of waterholes, an extreme measure to cut down on the population of brumbies, or feral horses, whose numbers were reckoned a threat to the grazing of cattle and sheep. Sir George pointed out in no uncertain terms to the Australian High Commission the flaws of this frankly idiotic policy: apart from anything else it was not only the horses but the native wildlife which would drink the contaminated water.

The League became involved in bullfighting, particularly in France, where injured horses were frequently patched up and sent back into the ring without proper treatment, and ILPH representatives took successful legal proceedings against bullfight promoters in both Toulouse and Agen.

As the 1940s drew to a close and a new decade approached, the ILPH had already expanded enormously overseas, and was now far more than an insular organization. It had contacts as far afield as Australia and Canada. It was working on the Transjordanian frontier, and in India, where suggestions for improvements in the management of horses in Delhi had been put forward to the government. It had worked in Iran, in Turkey, and in Ethiopia, where it advised on the management of the gharrie horses – a gharrie is a light cart – under the supervision of Haile Selassie's own veterinarian. It had contacts in South Africa and had overseen a shipment of horses from Mexico to Columbia.

In Europe, there were ILPH representatives in Eire, Northern Ireland, Scotland, Belgium, Denmark, France, The Netherlands, Sweden and Germany, where Herr Wilhelm von Braubehrens and Frau Magdalene Beleites were back with their pre-war sister organization, now called PferdschutzVereinigung über ganz Deutschland. Amazingly, in Berlin and among the ruins of Cologne, these dedicated people were out on the streets almost as soon as the war was over, checking the traffic in horses from Poland, which was struggling to rebuild its war damage. There was a saying at the time that the worst thing on earth to be was a Polish horse. They suffered abominably in the rebuilding of Warsaw. The same horses, then on their last legs, were exported to France for meat, and Herr von Braunbehrens would stop them in Berlin, to water them and feed them and generally try to make their last journey a less hellish one.

In 1950, the ILPH participated in the World Congress for Animal Protection, held in Holland and attended by delegates from thirty-seven countries. The ILPH representatives were Anne Colvin and her husband Mark, who made an eloquent and impassioned speech on the need not only for international agreement on the regulation of horses in transit but for the protection of animals generally. 'Probably the most important step forward taken by this Congress', he said, 'is in the direction of international co-operation and co-ordination of animal welfare.' He made the position of the ILPH clear: 'As an international League, and as staunch advocates for many years of international co-operation in our special subject of the transport of horses, and realizing from bitter experience the almost insuperable difficulties that confront us in the absence of international agreements, the League gives its hearty support to this venture . . .' Other resolutions he suggested included the protection of birds, the supervision of animal performances in circuses, and the regulation of zoos. He advocated the promotion of animal legislation and further laws to improve conditions in slaughterhouses. He suggested ambulance services for animals, studies of draught and chained dogs, the establishment of animal rescue homes, police protection of animals and the abolition of vivisection.

Out of this Congress came the World Federation for the Protection of Animals, afterwards renamed the World Society for the Protection of Animals (WSPA), with which the ILPH maintained links for many years. But, as ever, good intentions were not enough. For all the enthusiasm generated by the 1950 Congress, little happened in practice. For over a decade the combined forces of the ILPH and the World Federation for the Protection of Animals did their best to secure complete international agreement for a revised draft of Sir George Cockerill's Convention to protect horses in transit, now updated to include transport by air. Documents went to and from the Council of Europe: there was plenty of talk, but precious little action. In 1966, the ILPH reported, with thinly concealed understatement, that 'the ILPH Council does not disguise its opinion that it is time a sense of urgency was introduced into official deliberations'. It became clear that if it wanted to see practical progress made, the ILPH must continue to rely on its own resources.

There was a brief resurgence of co-operative action in 1975, when Charles Bennington, in conjunction with the World Federation for the Protection of Animals and the Canadian Wild Horse Society, launched a joint volley at the Canadian government which had once more allowed the resumption of shipments of live horses for slaughter across the Atlantic to France. This particular campaign was a success. Intensive publicity resulted in an effective ban on the export of all equines except duly certified pedigree stock. Shipments were not to exceed fifty in number, and no horses would be shipped from any port in Canada in the winter months, with their heavy seas, from November to March inclusive.

But as ever, for every victory won a new problem reared its head. In the same year the ILPH representative in Greece, Basil Acriviadis, was faced with a government decree which increased the number of ports open to the export of horses from two to sixty-one. Still, he proved equal to the task, and managed to monitor the traffic through every one.

It was not until 1979 that a truly effective international body – or at least a European one – began to emerge.

Eurogroup was the brainchild of two RSPCA men, Michael Kay, a past Chairman of the RSPCA Council, and Mike Seymour-Rouse, Director of European Liaison. For some time the RSPCA had seen the potential of what was then the EEC as a platform for the protection of animals in its member countries. Michael Kay said that 'my successor as Chairman of the Council, Roy Crisp ... had devoted a great deal of time to trying to form a European body capable of handling co-ordinated campaigning and lobbying. Unfortunately the time was not right to succeed then, and their efforts, while not wasted, did not bear fruit. They had, however, started to lay foundations ...'

By 1979, the time was right, and the newly established Eurogroup held its first plenary session in Brussels in March 1980. The key to the new organization lay in the fact that it embraced every nation that belonged to the Council of Europe – not just those that were members of the EEC. It was composed of one representative and influential animal welfare organization from each country, each organization having two delegates and one vote. Today it sits in Strasbourg, and Surgeon Cmdr. David Baker, Director of European Operations, and James Proven, European Lobbyist, present the ILPH case.

Eurogroup has undoubtedly helped to improve the conditions of horses in transit. As early as 1981 it showed results: the *Guardian* reported on 21 October that 'the parliamentary assembly of the

21-country Council of Europe voted unanimously yesterday to tighten rules on the humane shipment of horses for slaughter from Eastern Europe and Africa to Western Europe. The assembly recommended strict adhesion to previously adopted regulations and an extension of those rules to non-members, particularly the Soviet Union, Poland, Yugoslavia, and countries in North Africa.'

Gunter Muller, German representative to the Council of Europe, reported the 1981 initiative as follows:

I am sure that if horses could vote and were able to complain in writing to their local MP, the sufferings endured by those among them sent for slaughter abroad would long ago have become a memory of the past . . . For the present cruel arrangements – affecting up to one million horses sent to the slaughterhouses of Western Europe each year by boat, train or lorry, often under indescribable conditions – are not in any way inevitable nor, for that matter, economically sound . . . If we find that economic greed, or inert, obsolete habits violate common decency, then we must react. Perhaps we should all pause for a moment and think: What if I had been one of the horses . . .'

Surely that is the point. Perhaps we should. And it did seem, at last, as if practical steps were being taken as a result of a genuine will to act. But even today, the solutions are not that simple. Regulations are passed, agreements ratified. The problem is in making sure they are implemented and effectively policed. It is a nearly impossible task.

The number of horses transported across Europe by train and lorry has not lessened significantly since 1981, when it was reckoned that around 500,000 were imported into Italy and 350,000 into France alone. Italian Ministry of Agriculture statistics put the current figure of imports into Italy at 400,000 per annum, although private sources suggest a far higher figure.

And the horses that are transported from Eastern Europe and Russia to Italy travel long distances overland, the misfortune being that in the Eastern Bloc itself regulations for animal protection are either non-existent or woefully deficient. Without a common policy between them the disadvantages of each country's different laws become very apparent. For example, some states require cargoes to be sealed, while others do not, and obviously a sealed cargo cannot, even if it is a live animal, be fed and watered. On top of this some Western European countries, such as Austria, do not allow live cargoes over their soil, which while it may be laudable in itself means that trucks carrying horses may have to make a lengthy detour. And even if the truck driver wanted to water his stock, the whole situation is compounded by the trucks and their loading systems which make feeding the animals well nigh impossible. Unless the driver is unusually conscientious or has help, in the absence of specially constructed holding pens, his hands are tied. When he stops at an autobahn café, is he supposed to let his horses out to mill around and graze on the central reservation? And when he is ready to hit the road once more, how should he round up his horses, which by now will have tootled off to visit the neighbouring parish? Of course, being the magician he is, he whistles them back, and here they come galloping over the autobahn, then obediently run back up into his truck again, which is where they are all dying to be.

It is hardly surprising that laws are openly flouted because of their sheer impracticalities, and with the opening up of frontiers today checks are even fewer than before. In all events, the losers are always the horses, the upshot being that thousands – hundreds of thousands – still face a five- to seven-day journey without food or water.

For those on shipments from South America it is even worse. There may be fewer of them – a few thousand a year as opposed to the bulk transports from the East – but these horses stand for twenty-three to twenty-six days in the same place on pitching seas. There is no room to lie down. Bites and fights are common, and more serious injuries are caused by horses coming into contact with unprotected edges of metal in the ships' holds. Those that die are unceremoniously dumped at sea.

The main thrust of the work of the ILPH has been with horses in transport. In any of the reports you care to pick up, from the very first to the last, you will find a lot of space devoted to this issue. It's not surprising: it is what the ILPH was all about, the issue it cut its teeth on; where the whole idea began. Most of the legislation it has helped to secure has been connected with the traffic in live horses, and most of its thinking has been in this direction and continues to be so. In the mid-1980s, it sponsored a study by the Fédération Équestre Internationale into equine stress during transportation, in order to determine the least harmful conditions of travel for horses by testing responses and establishing the most beneficial routines of feeding and watering during transit. Its representatives work constantly to monitor the movement of live horses for slaughter and to inspect transatlantic shipments to ensure their safety.

It is a battle that is far from won. There is always work to be done. Ships nowadays are supposed to conform to a European Standard, but even so, pitching seas are not good places for livestock. Nor are the ships' crews or the dock workers skilled in handling animals. I have seen horses unloaded from ships in Italy by dockers standing in front of them and hitting them across the face with thick wooden canes to get them to go forward. Men lose their tempers, animals get terrified, and accidents happen – still.

TEN

The other main issue which occupies much of the ILPH's time and resources and is the spearhead of their work overseas is that of education. ILPH philosophy is not to preach but to teach. To anyone who travels it is obvious today, as it was in the fifties and sixties when the ILPH began seriously to work abroad, that in many countries a different attitude to animals and their handling prevails from what we are used to in Britain.

Who is right and who is wrong over the way animals should be treated is an endless debate, and those who use animals for work will inevitably see their function in a different light from those of us who don't.

They will argue that daily work with animals precludes a sense of sentiment that only those who do not have to work with them can afford, and that working animals are bound to be more often regarded as objects than animals born and kept in circumstances where their owners do not need to make economic demands upon them. If you have ever worked with animals that are used for draught purposes or production this will hold true. But it does not hold true, for instance, in a yard full of livery-horses used for hacking or driving, any more than it holds true for a yard full of expensive racehorses, simply because there is a subtle difference in these animals' standing which conveys a higher duty of care.

In general, we in Britain tend to treat animals well, and to regard them as worthy of consideration and protection, whether they are pets and companions or domestic livestock. However, it has taken us a long time to get this far, and our history is not blameless. Since we are not without sin ourselves, can we rightly claim to be able to cast the first stone? It's a difficult subject, since to believe that one has a fairer outlook on the treatment of animals presupposes a superior knowledge, and any assumption of superior knowledge can all too easily imply arrogance or undue criticism, particularly to those who use draught animals – who *depend* on their draught animals – a lot more than we do.

For us in Britain nowadays horses are things of pleasure, and are enjoyed primarily for sports or other recreations. Even when they are used for agricultural or draught purposes there is still an element of showmanship involved which suggests, at least, the idea of pleasure in their use.

In Third World countries, or even places such as Mexico or Eastern Europe or Russia, the horse is used for work. He is a beast of burden. Accordingly his station in life is greatly diminished when compared to the position which he holds in Britain. To anyone who uses a horse to earn his livelihood, the horse is no more than a means to an end to supply daily needs. He is definitely not a luxury. And since two-thirds of the world's population use animals for draught work, this is the light in which their beasts of burden will be viewed.

When, therefore, someone from another country pitches up and starts telling them how to look after their horses or donkeys or mules or cattle, what to do and what not to do, the chances are that that uninvited interference, those suggestions that they mend their ways, will be met with scorn, or blank refusal, indignation or even anger.

Yet, if on visiting some foreign place, we stumble across a man whipping his exhausted and starving mule, forcing him to pull an overly heavy load along some burning street, should we turn our backs and walk away? Have we any right to interfere? Should we say what we think, and *then* walk away? Or should we contact someone locally who may be in a position to help, and if this is the best answer, whom do we contact?

It is never straightforward, and this is paramount in the minds of the ILPH field officers, or any animal welfare officers for that matter: to discover the most effective means of getting their job done without incurring unnecessary resentment or bad feeling in the process. It is an area fraught with problems, and one in which the ILPH treads carefully, aiming always to demonstrate by encouragement the benefits of better treatment of draught animals rather than to criticize or condemn.

*

A friend of mine once told me a story. He was living at the time in the Bahamas, and driving along one hot summer's day through Nassau, he saw a couple of tourists in a horse-drawn carriage being pulled by two sweating, worn old horses. He stopped his car in front of the calèche, got out, went up to the tourists and asked them in a friendly manner if they were having a nice time. Yes, they told him, lovely. Then he pointed to the horses and said, what about them? They hadn't noticed the horses, they said.

Tourists *can* have an impact on the way animals are handled, either by not taking that horse-drawn buggy round the town, or by making strong complaints to their tour operators if they come across horses in poor condition. But even here the issue of conscience is not a simple one. By not taking the calèche you run the risk of leaving the driver's pockets empty, so that he, his family and his horses will go unfed that day because you, the tourist, turned him down. One always has to consider the other side of the coin. Most of these people live a hand-to-mouth existence, and no takings for the day can have acute consequences – and in such a case the animal will be the first to feel the pinch.

In its attempts to come to grips with these problems the ILPH has tried numerous approaches.

In Spain in the 1950s they funded a veterinary practice and brought about an immediate improvement in the local animal population. Funding meant that the practice could expand, employ more people and treat more animals. The real task, however, was to prevent the injuries or the mismanagement that had brought the animals to the clinic in the first place, and to this end the ILPH combined the two functions of the treatment of sick animals and education of the populace with similar schemes all over Spain. They set up stables in Valladolid, Seville, Málaga and the Canary Islands, and even had a presence on Majorca, long before that island became the honey-pot for tourism that it is today. To supplement the work of the stables, in 1959 they began to broadcast on Spanish radio, advising on simple techniques of equine husbandry in conjunction with the local SPCA.

Radio was also used in America. In 1959, the ILPH received a report from Kansas concerning the treatment of horses sent for slaughter there. A call from the ILPH in England to Kansas City Radio was broadcast over seven states. Response was immediate, a flood of letters arrived a week later at the ILPH offices from Kansas, Utah and Idaho, all in support of the stand the ILPH had taken. Their American correspondents also drew their attention to the plight of the wild mustangs, which were at that time being gunned down for meat in their thousands. The ILPH approached the British Ambassador in Washington and a sufficient stir was caused to keep the problem in the public eye until the Humane Slaughter of Animals Public Law No. 85–765 was passed by Congress later that same year.

Meanwhile, in Australia in 1960, the ILPH and the Australian RSPCA between them undertook to patrol race and trotting meetings, and in Canada the ILPH and the RSPCA secured the provision of helicopters to drop feed to a group of wild ponies – descendants of shipwrecked stock – on Sable Island, off the coast of Nova Scotia, which were starving because of the bad weather.

In 1959 in Italy, the ILPH held Cab Horse Competitions for the best-kept horse in the towns of Catania and Padua – these having at that time a large number of horse-drawn vehicles. This particular experiment proved a remarkable and instant success, since the prizes given were well worth having, and the standard of horse welfare improved dramatically. Drivers quickly found that cabs drawn by horses in good condition were more readily hired than those with poorer horses, and before long, without further persuasion, the well-kept horses had become their drivers' pride and joy.

In Spain at the same time, a Harness Fund was set up to provide leather coverings for the metal nosebands – often with serrated edges – which were in common use. These nosebands were similar to hackamores or bitless bridles, and this venture was less successful, since the kinder, leather-covered nosebands which inflicted less pain on the horses when pressure was applied to the reins, meant that the drivers found they had less control over their often inadequately broken and inadequately trained horses. Here was an example of the argument that brutality is frequently linked to a fear of loss of control – and one, moreover, which underlines the fact that a horse used to earn his owner's livelihood is unlikely to be treated as well as one used entirely for pleasure.

The following year a new scheme was tried in Italy, this time a special fund to award prizes to police with a good record in preventing cruelty to animals. Most of these cases concerned the excessive beating of draught animals; or the transport of animals in overcrowded conditions or without shade from the sun, or else in unauthorized vehicles. One related to a four-month-old foal carried on a Lambretta scooter with its legs tied together. And in Pompeii, several cab drivers were warned that their licences would be taken away if they did not take better care of their horses.

All these steps in Italy were implemented in conjunction with the Italian SPCA, which was run then by Mrs Catherine Brockhurst and Brigadier B. U. S. Cripps, a member of the ILPH Council, and between them the two organizations set up a mobile dispensary which covered the length and breadth of the country.

In Israel the first animal shelter was built in 1960 with ILPH funds by Miss M. R. Silverman of the Israeli SPCA. Later ILPH representatives in Israel included Dr Rolbag, MRCVS, the official police veterinarian, who implemented a scheme to replace the painful square-ported bits then in frequent use with kinder English snaffles.

Also in 1960, in Greece, ILPH funds enabled the first animal refuge to open in Athens, and a year later the ILPH and the RSPCA sent out to Greece two Rice Horsebox Ambulances and two Thames Transit vans to pull them, which were presented to the Greek Animal Welfare Fund on 26 September. Greece was the focus of considerable ILPH activity in the 1960s. Charles Bennington, then an honorary field adviser, spent a month there, touring markets, fairs and slaughterhouses, first around Athens and then in the north, studying conditions of equine welfare and advising on modern methods of slaughter. There he met Dr Chacalof of the University of Salonica Veterinary Department, an invaluable ally of the ILPH for over fifteen years. He and Bennington, together with Basil Acriviadis, ILPH representative in Greece, provided proper loading crates for the docks at Igoumenitsa and Corfu to replace the crude rope and tackle arrangements with which horses and mules had been hoisted previously. He introduced attempts to improve the local stock by using quality stallions – Thoroughbreds and Arabs. And it was Dr Chacalof who drew the attention of the Greek authorities to the execrable law which forbade the export of fit horses for slaughter. In practice, this law had resulted in the employment of a man on the docks at Igoumenitsa whose job it was to deliberately gouge out horses' eyes and break their legs with an iron bar to make them unfit, and therefore legally exportable.

In 1962, once again trying to improve the lot of working horses, the ILPH printed pamphlets on horse care in Arabic, which were distributed in the Lebanon. The same year they worked in Costa Rica with the local SPCA to improve the conditions of the mountain horses used for the transport of coffee. In Chile, with La Liga de Protección al Caballo and alongside the police, they repeated their successful Italian experiments – one of issuing rewards for the prosecution of overt acts of cruelty, and the other of awarding prizes for outstanding horse-drawn cab drivers. Here, after three years, they secured the first legislation to be aimed at improving the conditions of working horses, and even had an ILPH presence on the Chilean territory of Easter Island, the world's most isolated island.

In 1964, a shipment of Argentinian horses bound for India was checked by ILPH inspectors and representations were made to the Indian government complaining about the high loss rate at sea on account of the duration of the voyage. No further shipments were made.

In Uruguay they worked on the docks to improve loading facilities for the horses sent for slaughter. Where possible, as in this case, they worked from the inside, with the exporting agents rather than against them, realizing that where economics dictate, and the trade in live horses from a poor country to a wealthy one is a necessary evil, it is far better for such a trade to be open and properly regulated than for it to be driven underground and on to the black market.

In 1974, the ILPH sent aid and funds to Cyprus during the war there, set up a reward scheme for Turkish carriage drivers and at the same time renewed their efforts to improve equine husbandry in Greece.

Across the Mediterranean in Africa there had been sporadic involvement since the 1930s in South Africa and in what was then Portuguese East Africa. But it was in North Africa in the 1980s that the seeds of one of the ILPH's most significant and lasting overseas initiatives were sown. This was the Moroccan farriery and veterinary scheme, which since its inception in 1985 has benefited many hundreds of horses in Agadir and Marrakesh, trained over seventy Moroccan farriers and is at the centre of an ambitious education programme undertaken by the ILPH in conjunction with Walt Taylor's organization, Working Together for Equines.

It all began as a direct result of an approach by the distinguished BBC race commentator and journalist Peter O'Sullevan. While in North Africa he had been distressed to see the condition of the horses that were being used for tourism on the beaches of Morocco. They were undernourished, their saddlery ill-fitting and their feet, almost without exception, bad. Couldn't the ILPH do something about it? he enquired – something that would have an immediate effect. After all, it was rather up their street . . .

The ILPH response was swift. An investigative trip by Roger Macchia, Inspector General for Europe, and Andrew Faulds, field officer, brought a recommendation to the Council that a clinic be established in Agadir. Andrew Faulds returned to Morocco to set up and supervise the new clinic in February 1985, and in exchange Dr Laheen Rakioui, a Moroccan vet, came to England to study the working methods of the ILPH. John Goode, a farrier, went out to Agadir to demonstrate British methods to the Moroccan blacksmiths, a training programme was drawn up and a delightful letter arrived at ILPH headquarters from the City Council of Agadir:

To: The Director of the ILPH

Greetings.

It gives me pleasure to send you my warmest greeting in thanks for the efforts you are making to bring the City of Agadir within the scope of the ILPH. Agadir is greatly in need of your help so that its horses are in good health and under medical supervision.

Hoping this noble effort achieves the aims we all wish for.

Salaams,

p.p. President
signed, Rabati Ibrahim

*

Such was the clinic's success that not only were owners queuing up to have their horses shod there, but the ILPH obtained permission from the Ministry of the Interior to withdraw the horses from the beach and set up a properly run system whereby tourists would hire horses from the local riding stables – of which there were no less than twenty-two, all good ones, all within the environs of Agadir.

By 1987, an extension had been built and 790 horses were treated in that year alone. There were some problems – unexpected at the time, but thankfully neither permanent nor insurmountable. First the Moroccan authorities decided to assume responsibility for the clinic themselves, under the supervision of their own municipal vet, and Andrew Faulds's resident permit was withdrawn. Then Ali Bardoud, a Moroccan farrier who had been trained in Britain and America by the ILPH, found his newly acquired skills in demand with a member of the Moroccan royal family, and for a while his work at the clinic ceased.

Today, however, the clinic thrives. Ali Bardoud has returned to it, and undertakes a vital role. Training courses are held in Rabat and in Marrakesh, and trained farriers and trainees are brought together for the exchange of ideas and information. There have been additional courses for vets and veterinary students on foot care, farriery and lameness.

Ali and the WTFE/ILPH team work alongside the Society for the Protection of Animals Abroad (SPA, formerly SPANA), which has its roots in North Africa and runs seven refuges in Morocco, seven in Tunisia, one in Algeria and two mobile clinics in Amman, Jordan. Thanks to organizations such as these not only horses and the other equidae but also cats, dogs and camels are afforded a measure of protection. SPA/SPANA provides invaluable help to the ILPH; they themselves tend over 300,000 animals in Morocco and Algeria alone – mostly donkeys, by far the most common of the equidae in daily work in North Africa.

They work with the Ministry of Tourism in Morocco, with the *calèche* horses under the Katoubia in Marrakesh and in Capbon and Jerba Tozeur, Tunisia. They brand and inspect horses three times a year to enable approved horses to obtain police licences. During the African Horse Sickness campaign in recent years, they have run an inoculation programme in conjunction with the Ministry of

Agriculture, and now you see donkeys, horses and mules with Vs tattooed into their necks, signifying that the animals have been vaccinated against disease.

SPA gets things done by locals, and its refuges are run by nationals, under the supervision of a vet. In this they espouse the same philosophy that is central to all the work of the ILPH abroad: to encourage by example, and thereby to sow the seeds of lasting change.

ELEVEN

Many people have been part of the story of the ILPH around the world, and many individuals have contributed to its successes. But of all the men and women on its international roll of honour, one name stands out above all others: Roger Macchia. Macchia worked for the ILPH for fifteen years, from 1975 until his death in 1990, and he put the ILPH on the map in Europe as no one had before him.

Roger Macchia was born in 1922 in his grandparents' feudal castle in the region of Drome, France, where he spent his formative years. In the war he joined up with Marshal Pétain's Army of the Free Zone, which was disbanded by the Germans on their invasion. He was taken to Germany as a prisoner where, by the simple expedient of discarding his papers and acting dumb, he contrived to be returned after three months to work as a labourer on farms in the South of France. Once back on his native soil he escaped to the mountains where he joined the French Resistance and, with a number of friends, formed light-armoured units which seem to have been a kind of guerrillas-on-horseback, with whom he fought out his own personal campaign against the Germans until the Americans arrived.

Macchia seems to have been a natural soldier, and his background is military through and through. After the war he commanded a camel regiment in Beirut and a mounted regiment in Syria, returned to France after a couple of years to marry, and then promptly left to join the Foreign Legion, in which he served as a member of the French staff. In Morocco he served with the 4e Spahi and Les Chasseurs d'Afrique, both of which were native mounted troops, and ended his military career in Algeria.

Home once more, he set up an American-style ranch complex fifty miles outside Paris, with sixty horses, a bar and hotel, and it was around the time it began to occur to him that the settled life was not one which would suit him that he met Charles Bennington.

The two men got on straight away. In a sense they were kindred spirits. Both of them were direct, forceful men. They both liked to see results, they were both practical horsemen, they both acted wholly on their own initiative and both were loath to delegate, which is at once a vice and a virtue: vice because no one else knows what's going on, and virtue because the job gets done.

But above it all they both shared that single-minded quality which will increase a man's ability way beyond that of his peers. Simply, these two powerful characters knew and loved their work; and their work was horses.

Within an hour of their meeting Macchia had an offer of a job on a three-month trial period, and when those three months had elapsed, instead of being confirmed in his post as ILPH inspector for France, he had proved himself enough to be offered the position of Inspector General for Europe.

Macchia was not one to beat about the bush. He started by looking at both Eastern and Western Europe, conducting surveys on those countries with the highest horse populations. He visited each capital in turn and met government officials – cabinet ministers, heads of department, ministers responsible for policy decisions affecting animals in transit: he met them all.

Having sorted out who was who and sifted the information he had gathered, he set out to see what could be done. The EEC legislation at the time was based on 1962 orders and directives which had laid down basic conditions for the transport of livestock. The snag was that although these regulations had been implemented their abuse was common and flagrant and their enforcement rare. Nevertheless, Macchia referred the ministries of the Eastern Bloc to them, reminding them of their legal obligation to adhere to the status quo if they wished to continue to trade with the West.

They must have wondered just who exactly was this determined little man telling them what to do. Who did he represent? And where did he get his authority?

The answer was, of course, that he had no real authority, other than that vested in him by the ILPH Council who employed him and who had asked him to remedy where he could the abuses in live animal transport across Europe. But Macchia had an air of authority about him. He also had charm and charisma and a confidence in himself which few challenged. They listened to him, and he got his way.

The first country that he set about was the biggest: Russia. The action he took was simple and straightforward, though it must have taken a lot of courage. In 1975, he boarded a ship with a cargo of horses in Klepeda, Lithuania, and sailed with it to Le Trépot in France. What he needed was cast-iron information regarding conditions on board, and that is exactly what he got. He recorded methods of penning, feeding and watering of horses and made recommendations for their improvement. With this information he returned directly to the Russian official responsible for the export of horses and told him bluntly that either they altered the way they transported their horses or he would personally see to it that a complete ban on horses from Russia – to include sports horses – would be implemented on his return to France.

How much of this was filibuster or sheer brass neck can only be imagined, but, whatever power Roger Macchia held, the manner in which he delivered his lines was sufficient to convince the Russians that this shoot-from-the-hip ex-Foreign Legion Frenchman meant what he said.

Incredibly, they complied.

After Russia, he tackled Poland. Poland, in the early 1970s, exported some 80,000 horses to France and 120,000 to Italy every year. Ever since the end of the war, horses had been shipped from Poland in truly dreadful conditions, herded into trains bound for Carpentras near Avignon in France for a journey which took twenty-one days. Though there were grooms who accompanied them as far as the East German border that was it. From there on the horses were left to whoever took pity on them, unless they went via Berlin, where some of the old ILPH connections were still operational, in much reduced and far less effective form. The rolling-stock was often bullet-holed – literally – the wagons suffocating in summer and draughty in winter. Carriages were shunted into sidings for days on end where this tragic cargo was left sweltering in sunlight or freezing in snow until a new engine could be found to take them to their destination and eventual slaughter.

It is deeply disturbing to think that men can become so distanced from their work and so unburdened by any sense of responsibility that they can just walk away from a wagonload of horses and leave them unattended in some siding indefinitely. What kind of man does this? And yet they do it and go on doing it, time and time again.

Roger Macchia succeeded in getting the whole business stopped, for an entire year, while the carriages were replaced or repaired and the system of transport reviewed. In the meantime, horses were transported overland by truck instead, a far quicker journey.

In 1979, he was asked to join the Council of Europe as an adviser. This gave him additional powers, and the authority to inform the Eastern Bloc countries that as of that date, any non-EEC state or country was bound to comply with EEC regulations or risk having their freight turned back at the borders. They had no choice but to conform.

In one or two instances the legislation backfired. The Council of Europe had furthermore laid down that any defective vehicles found transporting horses would have their cargoes seized en route. And indeed this is exactly what happened. Cargoes were seized, and some were turned back – at terrible cost to the animals.

At that time there were no rest stations such as there are today, at Apach or Bebra, which were built after protracted discussion with railway authorities in 1980, at Macchia's insistence. He was also responsible for the establishment of specific routes from east to west with specific halts, and the upshot of his work is that those journeys that used to take nineteen to twenty-one days from Poland now take from three to five – which, when all is said and done, is still three to five too many.

Next Macchia turned his attention to Hungary, Poland, Romania, Bulgaria and Czechoslovakia and told them the same: conform to EEC rules or lose your trade. These countries were of course then still behind the Iron Curtain, and it is an enormous credit to Roger Macchia that he achieved so much under the additional difficulties and suspicions occasioned by a Communist regime.

And he did not stop there. He had all rolling-stock carrying livestock marked in some way in order to distinguish them easily from others, and that such wagons ran then, as they run now, with horse-head symbols painted on them is down to Macchia.

In Western Europe, in his home country of France, he set up an organization called CHEM (Centre d'Hébergement des Équidés Martyrs) which, like the ILPH in England, was to provide a sanctuary for neglected and abandoned horses. Today CHEM has over 600 horses successfully re-homed or out on loan and some 800 others in its care.

In Italy, Macchia secured a major victory. Italy was then, and still is, Europe's largest importer of live horses from South America, with 30,000 horses being landed every year from Argentina and Uruguay. Macchia, who had gone, as usual, in person to the Minister responsible, obtained the permission of the Italian government for an ILPH inspector to travel with every shipment. The role of the inspector was to check every ship prior to its departure, and any that failed to meet EEC standards would not be allowed to sail. He was to check the loading of horses and could even attend the initial selection of horses from the *estancias* inland. On board ship he was to ensure that hourly rounds were made of the horses, and, furthermore, in matters concerning the horses, he had the authority to have the crew act on his instructions.

This is a ruling which still holds good to this day. Some of Macchia's methods were unconventional. In Greece, he had a television crew pose as tourists and film in secret the loading of horses into ships at Igoumenitsa and Corfu. He showed the film to the Minister of Tourism and the Minister of Agriculture. This, he informed them, was a duplicate, and, unless the conditions it depicted improved, he would have the film circulated around the television networks of Europe. He was thrown out of Greece for this little episode but the handling of horses improved.

Sometimes the ILPH Council itself did not know what to make of him, and some of the comments in the minutes of their meetings make diverting reading. One from 1978 reports that 'General Macchia has a number of wild ideas. He is proposing to have manufactured plastic stickers to put on to motor-car windows to make further known the objects of the League.' And again: 'General Macchia has proposed this morning something which is more or less a world tour with the object of inspecting equines in every state . . .'

One is forced to wonder how much, if they had only given his vision and energy full rein, the horses in every state could have benefited as a result!

As it was, his ability to take immediate and decisive action may not have endeared him to certain people, but his legacy to the horses of Europe was never in doubt. Chris Larter, who works with horses in Jordan and back in the seventies ran a horse transport business, reported to the ILPH a scene she witnessed at Modane, on the French/Italian border, while travelling with the British show-jumping team.

We were kept waiting for twelve hours.

When we arrived we saw a lot of goods wagons at a siding, which were full of horses with no food, no water. They were still there when we left, still having had nothing to eat or drink. There were twenty horses and twenty ponies on a platform, which were eating a limited amount of hay before being unceremoniously bundled loose into wagons by five or six rough men who beat them with sticks. When I saw a man beating a horse over the head I could bear it no longer and yelled at him to stop . . . The other grooms who were with me, and myself, looked into the wagons. In each there was at least one horse who didn't agree with the others, and therefore a kicking match ensued, with sickening thuds and thwacks as bodies and legs were hit, accompanied by squeals, and gnashing of teeth. Being jammed together there was no way that the other horses could avoid being hit . . . In the next wagon we heard a lone horse pawing. I was suspicious as to why it was alone and why it was tied with a rope which reached outside through the window grille. I climbed into the wagon and discovered it had a completely shattered off-hind leg, which was swinging uncontrollably. The rope was tied around the poor creature's neck in such a way that at the first shunt the animal would have fallen and strangled itself. We undid this and gave the horse two bales of straw to lie on as there was nothing but manure under its feet. However, it proceeded to devour the straw, it was so hungry. When I asked for a vet to come and shoot it I was told there wasn't one, and that the horses were under customs, and we should leave them alone . . .

This information was telexed to Roger Macchia, who travelled at once to Modane and found conditions there just as Chris Larter had described. And thankfully, as in so many other places, he was able to do something about it.

But for me at least, of all the many things he did across the length and breadth of Europe, there is one which has a peculiarly symbolic significance. The abattoir of Vaugirard, on the outskirts of Paris, where so many millions of horses had met their hideous end, had been in some sense the grim birthplace of the ILPH. It was the scenes they witnessed in Vaugirard that drove Ada Cole and the other early pioneers of the League like Patrick Keatley, who wrote about it in the *Manchester Guardian*, to devote themselves to saving the horses which were bound for its gates. It was Keatley's graphic descriptions of the hell of Vaugirard that did so much to popularize their cause.

Roger Macchia had Vaugirard closed down. When he did so, he somehow managed to wrest from the slaughterhouse authorities the very last horse to have entered it, and sent him for safety and an honourable retirement to a friend, near Dieppe.

And that, for an old horseman, is a fair memorial.

PART FIVE

Towards a New Future: The ILPH Today

TWELVE

Nineteen-eighty-eight was a crucial year for the ILPH. Norman McLeod joined the Council, and to them he made the proposals that would fundamentally alter the organization. He asked them three basic questions: what are the objects of the ILPH? How can these best be achieved? And what is its future direction? He made his colleagues on the Council think – and then he offered them an answer.

He had in mind a complete new management structure, and a shift in the way the ILPH was run. What they needed, he suggested, was a Chief Executive. It was not the job of the Council to formulate daily, weekly or monthly policy, or to involve themselves in the minutiae of the day-to-day business of the ILPH. There was a need for new and dynamic leadership – and he had in mind exactly the man to do the job.

Charles Bennington, of course, had given them leadership, as Honorary Director – and before that as Field Supervisor – for twenty-five years. But he was by this time well into his eighties, and although his will to go on was as strong as ever, it was clear that an infusion of fresh blood was needed.

It can't have been easy for Bennington to hear this – if hear it he did: he was very deaf by then. It must have been difficult to accept a new structure superimposed on his, to watch his systems swept aside and new ones proposed in their place. Change is hard for us all, and is surely particularly hard when one has given the best of oneself, all one's thought and energy, to something only to see it taken out of one's hands and put into the hands of another. What did Charles Bennington think as he looked round the Council room that day? Did he feel as if everything he had worked and fought for was finished? Or did he feel that he was handing on the torch to the best of the new generation who would follow after him.

In any event, he agreed to work alongside the man who would take over the reins from him, to enable the new Chief Executive to learn the ropes, and it is testimony to the tact and diplomacy of the man they appointed that the takeover worked as smoothly as it did.

The man that Norman McLeod put forward to run the ILPH was Colonel George Stephen. Thirty-one years in the army had given him ample experience of both administration and command. He knew horses: he had ridden all his working life. He spoke French and Arabic, and in the course of his army career had come to know Morocco well – no small advantage at the time, since the ILPH were then deeply involved with the clinic in Agadir. All in all, his credentials were perfect, and the Council had no hesitation in recording the view that Norman McLeod had found them 'a splendid candidate who would be a great asset to the League'.

The appointment made, things moved swiftly from then on, and, as tends to happen when people are fired with a new enthusiasm, all traces of acrimony and disagreement were put behind them. In addition to a Chief Executive to carry the burden of strategy, they needed a General Manager to implement in practice what had been agreed in principle. The man they chose was Richard Felton. Like George Stephen, his background was military, and he brought to the job clarity of purpose and an innate ability to identify and focus on the right objectives. Norman McLeod was elected Chairman of the Council on the unexpected death of his predecessor, Henry Payne, and shortly afterwards made his second proposal for a new and more effective future.

Two years previously, the ILPH had bought Hall Farm in Norfolk to be the largest of its rehabilitation homes for horses. Charles Bennington had heard that it was for sale: it was practically adjacent to his own home at Overa. The farm was large – 542 acres – and work began at once to convert it for its future equine inhabitants. Fencing was erected, using the ILPH's own labour. Water was laid on to paddocks, buildings repaired and converted for staff use, furniture bought for live-in grooms. The storms that ravaged much of southern and eastern England in the autumn of 1987 had been a setback: several buildings that had just been repaired were damaged, and trees and fences lay about the paddocks. But at least none of the forty-two horses already in residence was harmed. Work began all over again, using, at the suggestion of Council member Dennis Beresford, local flint to reconstruct the buildings in traditional Norfolk style.

George Stephen proposed that the ILPH should relocate lock, stock and barrel to Norfolk, and have its Head Office at the new showpiece Hall Farm. It was an idea that made sense on every level. To close the London office – then in Camden – would both reduce costs and dovetail the whole administration. There would no longer be a division, actual or symbolic, between London and Norfolk, Head Office and farm. And in a sense it would bring the ILPH full circle, back to its spiritual home, since it was in Norfolk that Ada Cole was born, and in Norfolk that she began the work out of which the ILPH had grown.

This was to be a major move. Obviously it could not happen overnight, and the pace of change had become so fast that many other things happened in the two years before the formal relocation to Norfolk could take place. Richard Felton and Anne Colvin made plans for the computerization of the office systems. The new building which was to house the ILPH at Hall Farm was commissioned in April 1989, and by 1990 its construction had begun. In the meantime, Portakabins were set up as temporary offices at Overa to facilitate the transfer, and Jack Ritson, Richard Felton's assistant, drove up and down to London with vanloads of paperwork, all of which had to be sorted and filed, put on to computer or thrown away. Membership-records, legacies received, covenants paid or unclaimed – all the paraphernalia of a major charity had to be unravelled and then reorganized in those makeshift offices.

It was an exciting, exhilarating time. Other new faces appeared, among them Sue Blackett, who became only the second person to take the minutes of the ILPH Council in over sixty years. And 1989 saw a landmark in their work. Jean Peloux, ILPH inspector on the transatlantic crossings, reported that a ship had left Uruguay with 1706 horses on board and delivered every one to Italy alive. It was the first time that a shipment from South America had arrived in Europe without a single death.

And of course the main business of the ILPH – protecting horses – went on too. George Stephen had had to acquaint himself pretty quickly with the scope of the ILPH: what it owned and didn't own; whether its capacities were overstretched or understretched; who was who and what was what; the work of the field officers; its contacts and commitments overseas. It can't have been easy, with half the records at Overa and half at the London office, and all the business of the move going on around him. But he lost no time in getting to grips with the job. He visited Roger Macchia in France to find out about the ILPH French connection and how it worked. He met with Andrew Higgins of the Animal Health Trust to discuss the setting up of an ILPH scholarship within the AHT; he set up channels for the ILPH to lobby Parliament on matters of equine welfare. He moved into West Carr Farm, which the ILPH had acquired to double as a home for their Chief Executive and as an isolation unit in the event of any problems with the horses at the main stables at Hall Farm and Overa.

George Stephen grazes heavy horses – Percherons – on the land at West Carr Farm, and in a way it could be said that heavy horses have a special place in the heart of the ILPH. It was the heavy horses that Ada Cole first saw on the docks of Antwerp in 1911, and heavy horses that went on the ships from Ireland to the Continent for slaughter, and heavy horses that travelled to France from Poland for nineteen days by goods train.

It was heavy horses, redundant both from the land and from the roads, that the ILPH bought up in their thousands throughout the thirties, forties and fifties, and heavy horses who were among the first to crop the grass at Cherry Tree Farm. And today, it is the heavy horses of Russia, the Vladimirs and the Sovietskayas, which are sent to Western Europe by lorry, to the abattoirs of France and Italy.

But in England at least, the future of the heavy horse looks rosy. It was the oil crisis of the 1970s that turned the tide of fortune in his favour, when people like Geoff Morton, Yorkshire farmer who has never had a tractor on his soil, could demonstrate for all to see the virtues of his team of fourteen Shires. Horses proved themselves efficient, economic and ecologically sound. Not only did they not use fuel – or not fossil fuels, at any rate – but they were cheaper to buy than machinery, cheaper to run, and longer lasting. And they were popular with the public. Their resurgence has proved much more than a gimmick: twenty years on, not only do heavy horses pull the brewers' drays and farmers' ploughs, but they are increasingly employed by local authorities to work the land in rural forests and in city parks.

So it seems to me only fitting that the Chief Executive of the ILPH should be a heavy-horse enthusiast. I think also of Roderick Watt, legal adviser to the ILPH, who is – guess what? – owner of heavy horses and Secretary of the Percheron Society. I think of another good friend of the ILPH: Roger Peacock, a man of Falstaffian appetites, farmer and enjoyer of the good things in life, local Norfolk character without whom the county would be the poorer, and keeper of – guess what? – Percherons. He's your top breeder, and his horses are tended by one Jack Jubey, veteran horse-coper, master ploughman, and turner-out of horses right-royal-and-proper, who owns on his own account more heavy horses – two prize Suffolk Punches.

The new home of the ILPH at Hall Farm was completed well on schedule and named Anne Colvin House.

Unlike so many of its counterparts nowadays, it is a building which appeals from both inside and out. It has a natural feel about it, perhaps because the architect, Charles Morris, was careful in his choice of materials. Most of them are local: flint, brick and tile. The wood is unusual, however, being a 'green approved' hardwood: it's light and limewashed and blends perfectly with the rest of the building.

A band of flint encircles the outside and breaks the evenness of the honey-coloured rendered walls. Maybe it's because the whole complex is in proportion to its surroundings; because of the way the brickwork complements the flint and the paleness of the timber gives it an unforced and harmonious appearance, but it just doesn't look like an office-block jammed there in the middle of the country. It doesn't argue with the ancient flint church alongside it, nor does it fight for attention with the traditional farmhouse and original farm buildings behind. And it's a good building to work in: the atmosphere light, the scent of the wood lingering and earthy.

It was formally opened on 27 May 1991 by Lord Henry Plumb, and Anne Colvin, by then very ill, was there to see it.

One wonders what might have gone through her mind. One wonders if she thought back to the Old Horse Traffic Committee, and that single room at 11 Lincoln's Inn Fields, in which she took on the burden of Ada Cole's work at the age of nineteen.

Since 1927, she had worked for the ILPH, and it had only been her total physical incapacity that had forced her, in the end, to retire from active participation. A serious fall, which necessitated five major operations in ten weeks, had left her immobilized but mentally as lively and alert as ever. As her son Alan later said, 'For someone previously so active and now totally dependent on others, this was hard to bear'. For the last years of her life this brave and remarkable woman had required constant nursing, twenty-four hours a day, and yet, in Alan's words, 'typically of her, Anne never complained or despaired for herself. She had the determination, fortitude and courage to extract the maximum of enjoyment for herself and others from these last often difficult and painful years. To the end, her thoughts and cares were for those around her.'

Anne Colvin died not long after Charles Bennington, on 30 March 1992.

She knew that she had left her work in good hands. According to Alan, when she was no longer able to work herself, she was 'disappointed at her own inability to continue but delighted at being able to see the work continue under a splendid new Chairman and excellent management team'.

His address at her funeral included this tribute:

'... she devoted her entire working life to the cause – sixty-three years in all – often working fifty, sixty or seventy hours a week, year after year. Starting with almost no funds and no support, she faced and overcame challenge after challenge, setback after setback, with a dogged determination that all who knew her acknowledged to be her hallmark.

One might have thought that so much effort expended on her charitable work would have been at the expense of her family and friends. Not so. She found a way to pack two lives into one, by working late into the night and starting again in the small hours of the morning – not just occasionally, but as a matter of routine for all those years.

Thanks to her tireless devotion, the League and its work for equines strengthened and prospered. It is today one of the world's most effective international animal care organizations – a fitting and living monument to her work.

It was in the very midst of the move to Hall Farm that a situation arose which confronted the ILPH with all the old spectres of the 1920s and the 1930s and which tested the mettle of the new organization to the full.

A letter arrived from Mrs McIrvine of the National Equine Welfare Committee, in which she alerted the various equine charities to the fact that the proposals for the 1992 Free European Market would mean the loss of the minimum values system – the very thing for which Ada Cole and Anne Colvin had fought so hard. It was astute of Mrs McIrvine to have picked up the threat at such an early stage, and if it were not for her we might well be standing today on the dockside heckling the legal transport of live horses across the Channel to slaughter.

As it was, within hours, George Stephen had called upon the Council to ratify the ILPH's position to spearhead the fight for the retention of minimum values. It was an issue, as he said, which was fundamental to the ILPH's history and foundation. The battle to save our horses from the terrible overland journey to the abattoirs of France and Italy had once more to be joined.

However, the issues which had been so clear-cut in the twenties and thirties were not quite so straightforward in the Britain of the nineties. With legislation that had been in place in one form or another since 1937, the issue of minimum values had lain dormant in the public consciousness for many years. Public awareness had to be raised – all the old arguments needed to be repackaged and delivered to a modern audience – all the reasons why the recrudescence of the traffic was to be abhorred. It was an emotive issue – but the facts were very real. It had to be pointed out exactly what it would mean if that long-fought-for legislation should be scrapped and the minimum values system lost. Britain would be plundered of its wild ponies; old cobs and family favourites alike, if sold at market, could end their days in the far-off slaughterhouses of Italy, and there would be no safety net to prevent it.

And that was not all. Things had changed in other ways. There was no longer a Vaugirard. No horse had been killed with a pole-axe in a European slaughterhouse since the last years of the fifties. The trucks that transported live horses across Europe were vastly more advanced and faster than they had once been. Ships had similarly improved, and EC legislation was in place to secure the better trans-port of horses – legislation that the ILPH itself had brought about.

There was room here for a very big banana skin indeed. It was a campaign that would have to be carefully planned and orchestrated if it was to convince both public and politicians that in spite of the changed conditions of the nineties, the trade *must not* resume.

Most challenging of all, there were economic and political argu-ments to contend with. Was not the point of the EC a single, undivided market with the free passage of goods from nation to nation? And here was Britain, as it would seem to many in Europe, trying to shift the goalposts right from the start, over the minor issue of the transport of horses. The ILPH and its fellow equine welfare charities had not only to persuade the EC – they had first to persuade their own British politicians that this was an issue worth fighting for.

It was vital that the various charities involved should join forces and pull together. They needed to present a united front of concerted and co-ordinated pressure. And they did so: with the support of the British Horse Society, whatever their rivalries and private policy disagreements, every charity concerned – the ILPH, the RSPCA, the Horse and Pony Protection Association and others – closed ranks and stood firm.

*

They won the battle: but it was a close-run thing.

Harry Greenaway MP, who has fought long and hard for a number of equine causes, spoke in the House of Commons on the ILPH's behalf. He said, 'This House takes note of the European Community Document No. 7871/89 relating to the protection of animals during transport, and urges Her Majesty's Government to negotiate the adoption of acceptable regulations governing the standards of welfare, inspection and enforcement by member states after 1992, particularly those which would sustain the current arrangements relating to the export of live equines from the United Kingdom, and to state clearly that Britain will not agree to anything that would encourage a resumption of the export of live equines from the United Kingdom for slaughter.'

George Stephen met with the All Party Parliamentary Animal Welfare Group, and then with Ray McSharry, the European Commissioner in Strasbourg. He went armed with photographs taken by ILPH field officers of horses being unloaded in European ports, which clearly demonstrated the ineffectiveness of current EC legislation in practice, and the cruelty involved. It was a meeting that elicited sympathy but not much in the way of hope. Commissioner McSharry understood their concern, but the Treaty of Rome was a treaty sanctioned by all the member states, and he saw no alternative. He did not think their case was likely to succeed; the most he could promise was that more effective controls would be put on transport and the implementation of a policy of slaughter in the country of origin would be investigated.

Back home, a massive publicity campaign gathered momentum, launched in September 1990. Members of all the charities involved were urged to write to their MPs, and their Euro-MPs, stressing their objections to the live transport of horses. A video was produced, called *A Long Way to Die*, which was widely circulated in order to broaden the arena of debate. The issue became a platform to bring the entire question of the live export of farm animals for slaughter to the attention of the public of Europe as a whole.

Support in Britain was immense, aided by press and television coverage. A petition presented to Ray McSharry contained thousands of signatures. The campaign culminated in an Equine Welfare Weekend held in Hyde Park in April 1992, and among those who pledged their support were John Gummer, Minister of Agriculture, and Baroness Trumpington of Cambridge, now Vice-President of the ILPH.

In the end, the cumulative voice of protest made itself heard. A special dispensation was issued, allowing Britain a reprieve, and the retention – for the time being at least – of her Minimum Values Order.

Despite their victory, the ILPH and those who fought alongside it cannot afford to be complacent. They are well aware that the concession is only temporary, and the battle goes on. There is still a powerful movement in Europe to retain the business of the transport of live animals for slaughter intact, and the fact remains that Italy and France – but particularly Italy – will do their best to import live horses for as long as they can. They have all the infrastructure to do so. They have trucks and ships, they have trains, and huge new slaughterhouses. They own lairages, and have land set aside for keeping horses if necessary to suit market conditions and prices. In short, they are completely committed to the import of live animals. That horsemeat does not travel well or keep well, or will be rejected by the housewife if not absolutely fresh, is nothing less than a myth actively perpetuated by the importers. There is a vast investment in live transport in Europe which will resist change at any cost, and it will not disappear until European law finally prohibits and outlaws once and for all the transport of live animals for slaughter.

Such is the work of the ILPH today. When a major issue such as the minimum values crisis threatens, they must be ready and prepared to confront it. But there are hundreds of other day-to-day issues with which they deal and on which they must take a stand.

One which has arisen recently is the question of the treatment of the horse in sport. For example, when freak weather conditions at Badminton Horse Trials resulted in an unfortunate number of accidents, a cry went up to put a stop to the event, or any event in which horses could occasionally be injured. This is the voice of fanaticism, not the voice of reason, and the ILPH takes a very decisive line. To quote George Stephen, 'The ILPH is totally supportive of all horse sports, provided they are conducted under the strict welfare laws laid down and enforced by the relevant sport's ruling body. The ILPH supports the use, not abuse, of the horse, because it believes that the best future for the horse in this increasingly overcrowded world is in his close association with mankind, for the mutual benefit of both species.' In practical support of this principle, the ILPH has given a grant of £20,000 to the Animal Health Trust to assist in a major research programme into stress and fatigue in competition horses, with special relevance to the 1996 Olympics in Atlanta.

In Eastern Europe, undercover film crews are working to bring to light the problems that exist there. They are knotty ones. Since the collapse of Communism, rising prices and the breakdown of supply chains have resulted in increasing shortages, and as winter draws in, the sale of his horse for slaughter might be all that stands between a man's family and hunger, even though he knows that if he sells that horse, he has nothing with which to work his ground next year.

These are the decisions that face the Chief Executive of the ILPH every day: how should he approach this and problems like it? Should he send assistance to the horses of the Philippines, caught in a tornado – just such a request came in last year. Or what of the horses of the Easter Islands, and the recent appeal for help from La Liga de Caballo in Chile? What of the gharry horses, trapped amid civil war and famine in Somalia? What of the horses of Soweto? The list goes on.

As I write, the restructuring of the organization and its headquarters is almost complete. The Council has a new Chairman: he is Philip Billington, an international show-jumping judge and course builder, a member of the British Show-jumping Association's rules committee and of the British Equestrian Olympic Fund. He and Richard Felton have great hopes for Hall Farm, which they would like to turn into a centre of equestrian excellence.

There is a new Director of Operations, Colonel John Sharples, who commanded the Royal Scots Dragoon Guards in the Gulf War, and a new Director of Equine Rehabilitation and Welfare, Captain David Hunter, who had been an instructor at Sandhurst and had also spent a year with the world-famous Cadre Noire at the École Nationale D'Équitation in Saumur, France. The restructuring of ILPH (Europe) is in the capable hands of Falklands War veteran Surgeon Commander David Baker, who lives in France, is a multi-linguist, and has a firm grasp of the issues that concern the ILPH. Within weeks of his taking office, he established a firm agreement with the main shipping companies which transport horses from Argentina to adopt new proposals for the shipment of horses. He believes that since the trade exists, it is better to work with the shippers rather than against them, and to secure, with their cooperation, as good a deal as possible for the equine freight they carry.

Changes apart, though, the backbone of the ILPH remains the same. It is the people out there, in the field, both in Britain and overseas; the men and women whose commitment and vision make the organization what it is, and it is at them and their work that the rest of this book will look.

THIRTEEN

The field officer of today is both reporter and conveyor of information. He has at once to be both diplomat and detective; he has to be able to make complicated connections yet be thoroughly down to earth. His approach must be firm but not aggressive, he must be someone whose opinions can be sought rather than offered unasked, and he must be amenable to all types and all comers.

It's astonishing really that his job gets done at all.

Having been on a few errands with field officers, I have been amazed at the variety and complexity of some of the situations they face. No two of them are ever the same, which means that there is never any absolute precedent to base a decision on. The whole job is off the cuff, all the time.

In terms of man hours, the field officers provide by far the greater chunk of industry in the whole organization. Their week is not a five-day one, nor do they work a nine-to-five day. Their hours are not set; the distances they travel not predetermined; the cases they deal with not something which can be reduced to a time and motion study. Any of them, if prepared to do so, can be asked to travel overseas to investigate a case at the drop of a hat – as did Norman Brown and Geoff Baker, who were asked to make up a team including members of the International Donkey Trust and the RSPCA, and went to Villanueva de la Vera in Spain to report on the degradation of a donkey at the traditional festival there.

Even at home a field officer often has little idea of what he is going to face – he can be confronted by anything from Rottweilers to thugs by way of satanism (which has been linked to the ritual mutilation of mares in the south of England found with increasing – and alarming – regularity over the past ten years). Even as I write, Tricia Horne, who works in the ILPH Head Office, is on her way down to meet the ILPH field officer for the South to investigate these sinister goings-on in the Meon valley in Hampshire together with the Alton police. Tricia tells me she's taking with her, for protection, not a cosh or a truncheon – but a rosary, a clove of garlic and a Bible . . . just in case.

The field-officer system grew out of the work of the investigators of the sixties and seventies: men like Ronald Burchnell and Tom Banks, Roger Macchia in Europe and Mr Crowe of Ireland, who used to travel from Dublin to the Continent with shipments of horses and accompany them to the abattoir when they were unloaded. Some of these investigators did work almost exactly like that of the field officers today. Among the first were a Mr Bradshaw and a Mr Chilmead, who between them in the seventies attended local sales of New Forest, Exmoor and Dartmoor ponies, which were at that time an easy target for the meat buyers. In the New Forest, the ILPH worked closely with the Verderers – the official administrators of the Forest – and brought a successful prosecution against an illegal trans-porter, a victory which had a substantial impact at the time on other buyers attending sales there. On a previous occasion, ILPH vigilance uncovered a ring of French horse-butchers at the New Forest sales, when six French car registration numbers were checked through the ILPH office in Paris. The auctioneers were informed, the police and port authorities notified – and no export licences were issued to the overseas buyers as a result.

It's a system which has evolved and grown around the individual officers as each has joined the organization and more or less adapted their work to fit themselves. Today, fourteen field officers cover England, Wales, Scotland and Ireland.

Tony Schormann is the longest-serving field officer – and the longest-serving member of the ILPH staff – and I can't wait to get out to Dublin, to see his Finglas mob again, them and their darting coloured ponies, in and out of lifts.

Rick Amery is the veteran of the English officers, having joined in 1976, and one of his first successes was to improve conditions at the then notorious Southall market in the west of London. In his first year, Rick investigated ninety-seven complaints.

Ron Jordan joined in 1982, and no sooner had he arrived than he found himself checking not horses or donkeys or even mules but zebras – and some hybrids called ze-donks – when he prosecuted a zoo for wilful neglect and threatened them with exposure in the press – another useful string to the field officer's bow. It's interesting to chat to Ron about those days. 'Then, you know, the whole thing was like a family concern. It felt smaller and more self-contained, perhaps, in the sense that it employed fewer people than it does today, but by heaven we did our fair share.'

Dennis Murphy, ex-Superintendent in charge of the Metropolitan Mounted Branch, is now Head Field Officer Supervisor for the ILPH. Norman Brown, Deputy Director of the field officers, was previously Chief Inspector of the Manchester Mounted Police, and it was he, together with Ray Jackson, an ex-Inspector of the Manchester Mounted Branch, who wangled a couple of weeks' training for me with the Mounted Police, an experience for which I shall be forever grateful.

The field officers rely on public support and information, and every complaint referred to them by members of the public is followed up. In some cases the information they act on turns out to be wrong, or rather misinformed – which is a mistake I have made myself once, when I reported a horse I saw in what appeared to be poor condition left out on a moor. In fact she turned out to be a very old horse – thirty-seven – whose owner adored her, and the only reason she looked so poor was because of her age.

Perhaps she needed putting down: who knows? Perhaps at times we can all be guilty of cruelty, if that is what it is, in keeping an old animal alive, and not having it put down, simply because we ourselves are fond of it. Fondness for animals often has little appeal to reason. In the hills where I live there is a story of an old man who was so fond of his Shire, Mistletoe, with whom he worked the forests of Clun for nearly a quarter of a century, and with whom he shared his tiny home, that one March morning, after a long winter, both were found dead in the stable, a blanket over the horse, a rolled jacket beneath his head and the old man lying beside him in his shirt-sleeves, frozen.

*

Captain David Hunter is the ILPH Stables Manager. He runs Hall Farm in Norfolk, and has overall responsibility for some 800 horses which the ILPH has out on loan all over the country.

In this context, he sifts the field officers' reports as they come in, which they do every three months, and in them will be accounts of quarterly surprise visits to horses on loan, to which the field officers have right of access at any time. The field officer reports on the general conditions of the horse, its feet, whether it is at grass or stabled, and what it is doing: if it is being used as a hack, or as a show-jumper, or whatever the case may be. All this information goes back to David and Head Office together with general comments, so that the ILPH knows the whereabouts and condition of every horse that has been placed in its care.

If a field officer or David finds a horse that no longer has a decent quality of life then he will arrange for it to be put down, and it was in this context that Bill Vose, field officer for the West Country, arranged for me to go and see an old mare being humanely destroyed at Stephen Potter's abattoir just outside Bristol. I was in no hurry to witness it, but one should see what one writes about, and I watched this bay mare, a thin, quiet old hunter, being led towards the killing shed on a headcollar. She walked towards it inquisitively, the way horses do, and though there was a hesitancy in her step there was no fear. The fellow who led her didn't frighten or alarm her, nor set her nerves jangling, as some might. He led her well and with purpose, which is the right way, as anyone who has ever led a horse knows. Give them a whiff of doubt and you'll be hanging on to that headcollar while they back off, heads high, into the neighbouring county.

He walked her straight into a whitewashed and empty room where, as he laid a rifle against her head, she looked out across the yard, to the trees beyond, and they were the last things she saw.

I am certain she had no idea what was happening to her. The slaughterman had been gentle. All I would say is that had she been my horse, as old as that – too old for another long winter – then I would have stayed with her; it would have been my hand that led her there.

Mike Elwick is manager of Overa House Farm where he runs an RDA (Riding for the Disabled) scheme with the Mid Norfolk and New Buckingham Groups. His aim is to make Overa the RDA Centre within the ILPH, and school any horses that come in for whatever reason, then offer those surplus to requirements to RDA Centres around the country.

One of the biggest problems in the rehabilitation of a horse, according to Mike, is its prodigious memory.

'You can get over many problems, be kind in treatment, teach him new things and handle him gently. But press the wrong button and all that old information will come straight back. Rehabilitation only really works through great patience and understanding, and to train a horse thoroughly you must become equi-morphic: that is to say you have to imagine the way a horse perceives the world and see problems before they arise. You can't just go sailing into things head on, you must think horse.

'A horse is trained by his memory. All the complicated things he is impelled to understand and respond to are sealed in his memory. You can teach him halts and half halts and flying changes, or turns on the forehand at a word, or get him to lie down at the sound of a whistle. Then you can turf him out to grass for six months and when you bring him in, you will find he remembers those things better than you.

'Because a horse is naturally a vulnerable creature, he has to rely on his memory and with it his ability to associate freely: that is how he stays alive. And it is that free association which will make a horse that has been abused always difficult to correct.

'In the ILPH we deal with equidae from miniature Shetlands to socking great Shires, from ze-donks to voiceless mules. And if a horse or pony is offered to us he might well be homed on the spot by the field officers without my having to be involved – after all, the field officers are highly qualified horsemen and they don't need me to check up on their work.'

'Obviously only suitable horses or ponies can be re-homed; those whose memories have not been permanently scarred by unpleasant or unfortunate experiences. The Loan Agreement which is drawn up between any potential borrower and the ILPH is a strict and lengthy document which sets out the most stringent conditions that must be met before the horse in question is allowed out on loan. New homes are rigorously vetted by ILPH staff and borrowers must satisfy me or the field officers that the required standard of facilities and care can be met.

'Some requests to borrow a horse can be very specific: for example, I looked at one for a fourteen- to fifteen-hand weight carrier with a sensible disposition, to be used for disabled riders. The address at which the animal is to be kept is required, together with a description of acreage and grazing. Then, before anything goes any further, the field officer in the area will inspect the potential site, talk to the potential owners and assess their knowledge and ability to look after the horse. Once all is in order the horse is in turn inspected by the borrower and their compatibility checked, and if all looks well, the borrower can take the horse away.'

In some cases horses are donated to the ILPH. These come in for a variety of reasons, not the least of which is through the break-up of marriages or through family disagreements, in which case, rather like the children, the horse becomes the victim of a tug-of-love, and without employing the wisdom of Solomon by offering to cut the horse in half, the situation can be resolved by gifting him to the ILPH.

Or sometimes the ILPH is offered a horse which, for one reason or another, proves unsuitable for its present owner. Recently a Highland–Thoroughbred cross was offered to them which had had extensive treatment for an occult spavin in the offside hock. As a result, the mare had a curious gait, and her owner, having suffered a bad fall and a back injury, could no longer cope with her awkward movement. Rather than have the horse put down, her owner chose to gift her to the ILPH. Ron Jordan's report reads:

I inspected the mare today and found her to be in excellent condition. Had I not been informed of the problems with the off-hock I would have said she was perfectly sound . . . I gather this animal is able to do reasonable work without any difficulties being encountered. I have been asked by Mrs X of King's Lynn for just such a pony, and the owner suggests that this animal may be very suitable for such undemanding work with the RDA (Riding for the Disabled). I personally suggest that we accept this mare. It is entirely possible that she should go directly to Mrs X . . .

The owner of the horse has enquired whether she could borrow a similar animal from us that would not cause her any back discomfort.

The pony duly went off to her new home where I understand she is doing her job beautifully. And her former owner was found a new horse to suit, one which caused her no back pain.

Some requests have caused raised eyebrows. Mike was startled to receive this missive from Robin Porter, field officer, who wrote: 'On 21 February I went to X Farm, Leighton Buzzard, where I met Mr Q, who requested to gift a 16.2hh 12-year-old Thoroughbred bay gelding known as Shergar ...' Not only was the horse the same size, colour and age as his famous kidnapped namesake, but the report went on, '... apparently this horse has a number of wins to his name ... and was the subject of an insurance claim where full compensation was expected although I understand that the insurance is likely to have lapsed ... therefore with the Insurance Company's permission ... and since Shergar is too old to race, he is offered to the League ...'

The ILPH is fortunate to have Roderick Watt as its solicitor and legal adviser. Roderick breeds Percherons, and like all owners of heavy horses, should you telephone him to clear up some point or other you have to wait a long time before the phone is answered, because he'll either be out repairing a fence or mending a ploughshare or thumping a spoke back into the wheel of a dray, or he'll be discussing the finer points of breeding, or dealing with a blacksmith or out on a baler, mouthing a yearling or littering down a barn.

And when not doing that, or employing his considerable brain on tort or jurisprudence, *res mancipatio* or the manumission of slaves, Roderick gives talks and seminars to the field officers on subjects related to animal welfare, the law, and what constitutes cruelty under various Acts such as the 1911 Act which he describes as '... an unfortunate piece of drafting, and difficult to unravel'.

Interpretation of the law is of course of vital importance to the field officers, who have to be able to assess a situation as they encounter it and not rush to conclusions or see things that are not there – which is easily done. They must know what cruelty or neglect is in terms of the law, which is knotty, since although it might on the face of it seem easy to recognize cruelty or neglect, every field officer in the ILPH will tell you they receive more complaints that turn out to be emotive and unsubstantiated than any others. But, having said that, I am certain they would sooner be informed, and find the situation to be under control and no cause for alarm, than not be told at all, and have horses and ponies suffer as a result.

FOURTEEN

In 1992, the ILPH was approached by Betty Svedsen, of the International Donkey Preservation Trust. The IDPT had been working in Mexico, and in the market of St Bernabe, the wood market of Capulhuac, and on the municipal dumps, they were seeing large numbers of horses and ponies in distress or in urgent need of treatment. But their charter allowed them only to work with donkeys, and, so to speak, their hands were tied. Betty Svedsen asked George Stephen if the ILPH would join forces with them in order to help the equines of Mexico. Out of this initiative, Working Together for Equines (WTFE) was born, and this chapter is its story.

But I'll begin with Walt.

Walt Taylor is a very fit fifty-nine. He's slim and muscular. He doesn't drink at all and is the kind of man who considers a question before he replies; and when he replies he looks you clean in the eye and you notice then that he doesn't so much speak as drawl in a slow Colorado brogue.

He was born on a dirt farm in the Midwest and grew up with horses the hard way. His father put him to work on the land as a youngster and that's where he stayed, earning his keep. I asked if it had made him a loner. Turning a ring on his finger he replied, 'A loner? Didn't think there was anything else.'

Since 1948, he's worked on a dude ranch in western Colorado, done the rodeo circuit, worked in a sawmill, even got a job as a prize-fighter before becoming a forest ranger. In his time he's been a cowboy, broken broncos, trained mules and taken people out trail-riding for days, nights or weeks on end. He told me a story about one of these trail rides. It was about a guitar.

He once had the job of taking a bunch of rich kids off on a long ride, and he baulked at the idea of taking their guitar. 'No place on a horse for a guitar,' he drawled. 'No place on a mule: no place on four legs.'

But they whinged and whined and begged him, and then they carped and grumbled and said either they took the guitar or the ride was off. And since the rides were his livelihood, Walt found himself cornered.

He rode pole, right out in front, sick at heart at the thought of this useless thing strapped on to the back of one of his string mules, annoying it, taking up precious space. He resented the awkwardness of it: the thing was nothing but a pain, and he resented the kids for bringing the stupid thing along.

The kids behind rode in a long procession. They were quiet enough and they didn't fool around annoying the horses as he'd feared they might. They didn't cause any trouble and they rode reasonably well.

That night they struck camp out in the open beneath a cloudless sky. The mules and the horses were tethered, a fire lit, coffee made and as the moon rose one of the kids picked up the guitar.

'You know,' said Walt, 'that was the darndest thing: they could play that guitar. That night they sang all the old folk-songs and cowboy tunes I grew up with – everything. They took me back to times I'd clean forgot, times when I was a nipper, when those songs were the only things I knew, the only things I had. Sure, they brought back old memories to me. That trip was the best I recall.'

Walt told me that story while we were standing on the municipal dump just outside Mexico City. It was strong sunlight at the time and the stench from the rubbish was thick in the air: flies were buzzing, and ponies whinnied occasionally while his farriers, his trainees, cut feet and tapped on new shoes.

Walt stood beside me in his jeans, leather apron and T-shirt. He was banging a rasp lightly into the palm of his hand, having just shown one of his farriers how to 'get that foot just so . . .' He seemed in the mood for talking and so I listened and watched as he drew angles in the dirt with the toe of his boot.

Of the farriers in America, he said they were 'about as communicative as a bunch of rocks'. It draws the strong, silent types, 'dead

Above: Many hundreds of fit and healthy horses like this shipment of South American Criollos, photographed by ILPH Inspector Jean Peloux, end their lives in the slaughterhouses of Italy

Left: Herds of Criollo horses from the pampas of Argentina are driven on to the docks of Montevideo en route to slaughter in Italy

Above: Dying horses litter the deck of a South American livestock freighter about to dock in Europe

Left: Horses that die on the long journey from South America to the slaughterhouses of Europe are unceremoniously dumped at sea

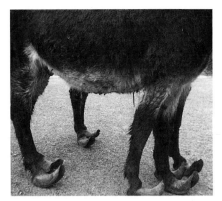 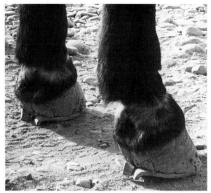

Above left: Neglect. Feet as overgrown as this make it impossible for the animal to walk. These are not Third World donkeys – they were rescued in England

Above right: Raised-heel shoes like these are common in the Third World, and force the horse's weight on to the front of the hoof. The cracked feet show evidence of malnutrition, and the white rings around the pasterns are hobble burns

The WTFE team in Morocco show off an example of good farriery. Left to right: Tina MacGregor, Walt Taylor and Ali Bardoud

Left: Despite a badly healed broken foreleg, this mule in Morocco is still in work

Below: Tony Schormann of ILPH Ireland feeds an orphan donkey foal in Stepaside, Dublin

Before and after: this pony in the care of Mike Elwick at Overa House Farm has made an excellent recovery

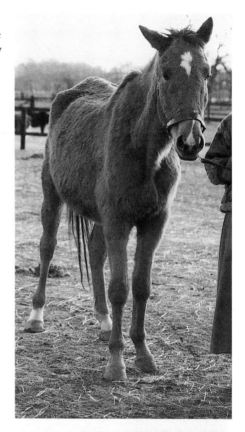

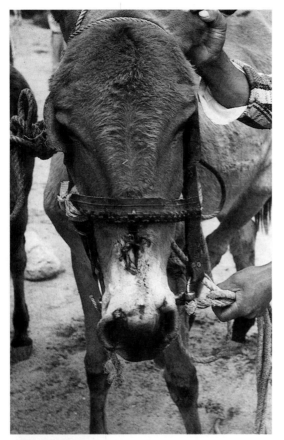

Makeshift treatments can sometimes do as much damage as the injuries they attempt to mend. The open wound in this mule's muzzle has been crudely stitched with wire

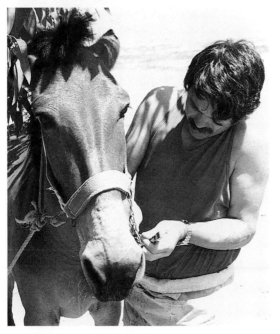

One of the lucky ones. This mule in Jordan has the benefit of a new webbing headcollar fitted for him by ILPH saddler André Bubear

Proper loading crates donated in the 1960s replace the crude and dangerous rope slings used previously at Igoumenitsa, Greece

Colonel George Stephen, appointed the first Chief Executive of the ILPH in 1988

obstreperous buggers, obsessed with the idea that someone was out to steal their business. Sure, it drew the loners, the outside guys.'

Guys, I suppose, a bit like Walt.

Then he told me another story.

He began it with reserve, the way a man does when he's not certain whether his listener will get the point, because it's subtle, and he knows that whereas the story is packed with moment for him, for his listener, it might not be. When a story comes like that you know that for its teller it was a touchstone, an incident that led to a change in his destiny.

It concerned one single horse, and it was simple: hardly a story at all. While he was shoeing one day, a horse suddenly lashed out and laid Walt out flat. That kick cost him forty days in a hospital with peritonitis, a ruptured pancreas, damaged spleen and kidneys. He never said so, but a colleague told me later that there wasn't much hope he'd pull through.

He shook his head and smiled and looked past me out across the dump. 'That was some ornery horse,' he chuckled. 'Yep, he was a real ornery horse.' He was quiet for a moment, gave the file to one of his farriers, pushed his hands into the back pockets of his jeans, and stuck his chin out at the men sweating in the sun. 'I keep telling these guys, "one day you'll get hurt". It's not a question of if, it's when, and how hard.'

That kick put Walt out of action for six months, and it was in those six months that he got to thinking.

He thought that there must be more to life than what he was doing: more to horses than just shoeing them or riding them or breaking or judging or whatever it may be. He had had plenty of experience with horses: more than most. He was a good farrier and knew it, and suddenly he saw the limit of his horizons. 'Kind of a Road to Damascus thing, you might say. Yeah. It all started because of that son-of-a-bitch ornery horse.'

Up to that time he'd been earning $100,000 a year shoeing horses in the States with a good head of stock, shoeing them on a two-month rotation. He'd always been interested in the exchange of ideas and the development of farriery as a profession, but the lack of communication between American farriers frustrated him. He knew that the only way to cut through that wall of suspicion was to put the whole business on a professional footing. He established the American Farriers Association, of which he was President for the next sixteen years. Then another idea formed in his mind, and a number of coincidences threw things together.

Walt had been contacted by a few people outside America who had shown interest in the way his American Farriers Association had developed: how it worked to exchange information and promote new, dynamic methods. In 1985, in conjunction with colleagues from Canada, England and Japan, the World Farriers Association was formed.

This was a visionary organization with ambitious aims. They wanted to improve the education of farriers worldwide, to provide a pool of expert advice and counsel, to assist the formation of national farriers associations, and to encourage international trade and exchange of materials, methods and expertise – especially in under-developed countries.

It was a wonderful idea – but there were problems. The founder members were all fully occupied with their own businesses. There were language difficulties, and logistical problems, and huge funds were needed in order to get the thing off the ground. The plans were there and the skill was there – but the time and the money were not.

There was no doubt the concept was a good one, but the funding was a nightmare and probably the whole thing would get wound up before it had begun.

And then Walt met Tina MacGregor.

Tina had come to the ILPH from the Royal School of Veterinary Studies in Edinburgh. In 1987 she had been involved in a new Scottish Training Centre for the Worshipful Company of Farriers, to which the ILPH had contributed funds for the buildings, tools and forges, and when the centre opened she was appointed full-time lecturer there in therapeutic farriery, paid directly by the ILPH.

Tina first met Walt when she went to America to give talks on footcare. It was at Louisville, where both of them were giving papers, that he outlined to her the aims of the World Farriers Association, which at that stage looked like being no more than an impossible dream.

Immediately, Tina saw the potential: that nugget of opportunity. She might know someone, she told him, who would be interested in his work. Back home, she put the idea to George Stephen. It was a chance too good to miss. A joint strategy was worked out with the ILPH, the Royal Society of Veterinary Studies and the World Farriers Association, and a name chosen for the new venture; a name which quite simply summed up their goal: Working Together for Equines. 'Never before,' they announced, 'have three different organizations collaborated in such a positive way to focus the world's attention on the importance of good footcare and farriery to the health and welfare of the equine. With improved health and productivity will come a profound social and economic benefit to the quality of life of people who use, enjoy and depend upon these animals . . .'

The briefest glance at the key points of the WTFE programme shows how wide-ranging is the job they have undertaken. It incorporates the original aims of the WFA: the worldwide exchange of ideas and information, the formation of national farriers associations, the provision of reference material, educational material, contacts, addresses, leaflets, videos and films. They plan international seminars, symposia, workshops and demonstrations that will bring together farriers, vets, horse owners and users to learn about and to face the very real problems that exist. And, most important of all, they have set themselves 'to develop and conduct training programmes . . . in various selected countries, specifically training people who will continue to practise the skills and who will teach others.'

The ILPH had already established contacts in Mexico, thanks to Betty Svedsen and the IDPT, when the WTFE began work there. A local vet, Dr Alfredo Lopez Cabanas, had been employed and vital links forged with the School of Veterinary Medicine at the University of Mexico City, through the offices of Dr Aline Aluja. Dr Aluja, a Swiss married to a Mexican professor, has worked on behalf of animal welfare in her adopted country for many years, and without her unfailing support and assistance none of the advances made by WTFE, by the IDPT and the ILPH, would have been possible.

Walt and Tina's WTFE training programme is strictly hands-on.

151

Local villagers who have shown an interest are given board and lodging by the university and trained by Walt and his team. The initial training course takes a month. The first week consists of lectures and theory, and in the second week the trainees practise on dead feet from the slaughterhouses and study anatomy and physiology. In the third week they practise on live horses, and in the fourth they visit the surrounding areas under supervision and begin to ply their trade. Each successful student at the end of his course receives a certificate to prove his training from the ILPH, the IDPT and the University of Mexico City.

An English-trained farrier might throw up his hands in horror and protest that proper training, as in England, takes three to four years. I put this argument to Walt. 'Sure it does,' he said. 'But we just can't spend three to four years training one guy for one or two days a week and send him out with another guy until he's got the business. What we try to do is recruit intelligent and enthusiastic guys in the first place and give them really intensive training. After that they are on their own, and sure they will make mistakes. There's no denying that. But tell me one farrier who's never made a mistake? Even with those mistakes they're so much better than what was going on before, they have a far better knowledge and understanding of the mechanics of the foot than any of the other local farriers – hell, they're doing a great job.'

He's right. I saw it for myself. To be honest, a lot of the feet cut were not cut perfectly. But as Walt said, they were infinitely better than what had gone before. You could imagine the donkeys sigh with relief, and see the horses smile.

Mexico is only the beginning of their work. Walt and Tina have given papers in Japan; they have set up in Jordan in conjunction with SPANA, and in Jamaica. There have been applications from Finland, Tunisia and Algeria, and a training programme is planned in Turkey in conjunction with Lord John Scott, whose father the Duke of Buccleuch was former President of the ILPH. The government of India has established a Centre for Equines at Hisar (Haryana) in order to improve horse husbandry in Northern India, where people have no other mode of transport. Already Walt and Tina have been there to do preliminary studies in breed improvement, nutrition, parasite control, farriery, footcare and general equine medication.

The world is their oyster and soon they will either have to clone themselves or expand their organization in order to meet the demand for their aid. They are popular and liked wherever they go, and no doubt this is because of their particular approach.

Neither of them has ever set out to undermine existing practices. All they have ever done is to show the people of the places in which they work an alternative way of doing things, one which invariably is quickly seen to be an improvement. Walt puts it like this. 'The reasons why horses, donkeys or mules are shod in the way they are usually results from traditional methods, using traditional tools, techniques and justification for producing certain results. In the case of farriery, the kind of equine and what it is used for add other dimensions to traditions. At "year one" sound reasoning may have gone into the decision to do things a certain way. Just as easily, a practice may have evolved because certain kinds of material may have been available at one time, but not another. Or, some unknown factor dictated that a job be done a certain way in one instance, but that one-off practice was copied by another who did not know the reasons for its being done in the first place. Following work may have been done after the same fashion, and further copied by others who applied it to their work. Thus are traditions born and their genesis lost to future generations.'

I daresay Walt has got as close to the truth as one can get, and one thing is certain: by understanding convention and tradition, and respecting it, one extends the hand of friendship, and the offer of help that follows is far more likely to be accepted.

André Bubear does harness work for WTFE, and his experience proves the point. André has been working in Jordan, from which he returned recently with photographs of the miserable saddles and headcollars, bits and bridles that are in everyday use. His philosophy is simple. He mends or makes what he can on the spot by buying local materials as cheaply as he can in local markets. From such easily obtainable materials he makes simple, comfortable headstalls. At first he amazed people. He amazed the locals by using materials they might not necessarily have thought of using, such as wide cotton webbing, which he says is cheaper than anything else and makes perfect headcollars. They had been using the webbing for beds. Now, they are copying André, and making their harness from it, and the problems of the damage done by the old-style wire headcollars has been reduced at a stroke.

And in the end it is not only the horse, mule or donkey that benefits. When you improve the health, and therefore the efficiency, of the animal, you increase its owner's ability to earn money. That in turn improves the standard of living for himself, his family – and his horse – and that again increases his self-esteem.

I saw it myself in Mexico. There was a young fellow there who had been taken on as an apprentice the previous year. He had been down on his luck – destitute. Tina said he was very withdrawn, and it took a bit of time to get him going.

This year the same young man employs two people whom he is training as apprentice farriers. He looks after sixty expensive horses and a whole gamut of village ones; he has saved enough money to buy himself a second-hand van to get around in. And apparently, he's caught the eye of a local girl and there's a wedding in the air.

PART SIX

All in a Day's Work

Even in the 1990s, even down the quiet and narrow lanes of rural Norfolk, even into the calm and businesslike offices of the ILPH, the violent shadows of war can still sometimes intrude when they are least expected.

About the time I began to research this book, civil war broke out in what had been Yugoslavia. Old wounds sprang open, and terrible stories began to filter into our newspapers and on to our television screens. There were stories of atrocities, and of the destruction of beautiful medieval cities. The hideous term 'ethnic cleansing' became unpleasantly common currency.

Into the midst of all this came a story about horses. An article in the *Daily Mail* was accompanied by a dramatic picture of a large group of horses being driven over rolling countryside by tanks. As it happened, it was a still from a film called *The Miracle of the White Stallions*, about the evacuation of the Lippizaners from the state studs of Yugoslavia by US troops from under the noses of the Nazis in the Second World War. But despite the fact that the photo referred to another war, fifty years earlier, the story was the same. The Lippizaners were once again at risk.

These were no ordinary horses. These were horses that had been raised on the same ground since Roman times, distilled into one of the most famous breeds of Europe by the Austrian Archduke Karlo in 1580. That's some pedigree. And there were precedents: they'd been evacuated before, and not only in the 1940s but also in 1797, to prevent them from falling into French hands, and again in 1809 and 1915.

That *Daily Mail* article was the catalyst. Suddenly, telephone calls poured into the ILPH headquarters. What did the ILPH propose to do? Why couldn't a truck be sent out with relief supplies, food, veterinary equipment – something? Donations came in – unasked for – for a self-invented Lippizaner fund. There were extraordinary offers of help: somebody rang to say they were greasing up their horsebox in readiness to help evacuate the horses, and yes, they were fully aware of the dangers, but the horses . . . the horses.

I happened to be at Hall Farm at the time, where the staff of the ILPH found themselves wrestling, on a smaller scale, with the same dilemmas that exercised the United Nations and the governments of Britain and America. How could we help? Should we get involved at all? Was it any of our business? How might it be viewed in retrospect? Might we inadvertently end up helping the wrong side? Which *was* the wrong side, and which the right? And what were we trying to achieve exactly? Was it really in our brief to enter war zones to rescue horses? Or was it idiotic even to contemplate such a mission?

Then someone – I think it was Jack Ritson – cut through all the indecision with a single statement: horses are horses, irrespective of breed or nationality or colour, and if these horses were in trouble and if we were in a position to help them then that was that: there was no need for further discussion. On the ILPH Declaration of Trust Deed, the third schedule, first paragraph opens: 'The ILPH exists for the worldwide protection and rehabilitation of equines. This is achieved through 1. Rescuing and rehabilitating equines found to be at risk . . .'

It was a clear mandate, but one problem still remained. Every report that had come in contained new inaccuracies, new contradictions. Some said that 300 horses had been killed, while others reported the number as ninety. Was there any truth in any of these stories? Were they authentic, or were they hype, mere propaganda?

What was needed was accurate information. Then a fax arrived which read: 'The Croatians say the (Serbian) army has deliberately launched whole volleys of artillery fire directly into the stable complex (at Lipik). Many of the horses died. Others broke loose and fled, with about three hundred horses escaping . . .'

Within three hours of that fax arriving, George Stephen was on his way across Europe. I went with him.

While George and I thundered across the Continent by car, Mike Elwick packed a horsebox with veterinary and other supplies, and Jack Ritson, who was to drive it, planned routes, made rendezvous points and picked himself a team.

Thirty-six hours later, George Stephen and I crossed the Austro-Hungarian border. In Budapest we made our way to the Military Attaché's office at the British Embassy, where the attaché – who asked me not to reveal his name – said to us, 'You are big boys now. If you go into Croatia you might well get away with it. Then again you might not. I would, however, simply add that we would advise against it, and regard the situation as extremely dangerous.'

By six o'clock that night we were in a small town called Harkany, hard on the Croatian border.

In Harkany, we learned that the State stud at Lipik had been wiped out by the Yugoslav Federal Army. The front battle line had moved through it and the fighting had been house to house. Not a building was left intact. The stable itself was burned out, empty.

Later we witnessed the damage, and heard about the horses, how they had been fired on, and that every one had gone, the survivors stolen and the remainder buried on the edge of a football pitch, in a little place called Filipovac, a mile or so away. We were told that the stable manager, a Serb, had stolen the best of the horses and disappeared with the stud books the day before the stud was shelled. We heard this information in a very guarded manner – this was, after all, war, and these were precious horses, worth a great deal of money. We heard it from Attila Mateus, a young man who had in his possession six Lippizaner stallions which had been among the first to be evacuated: they had come from a stud in Djakovo, some thirty kilometres from Vukovar, thirty kilometres behind the front line, and there were still more horses there.

That evening George Stephen and I stood on the battlements of Siklos castle, a tall, grey Austro-Hungarian fortress aloof and high above the windswept river plain that divides Hungary and Croatia. In the distance was the dull crump of guns, the sporadic rattle of machine-gun fire, with the occasional streak of tracer fire arcing the sky. Beneath the sound of the guns was another noise, a sharper, popping sound. Colonel George had his hands thrust deep into the pockets of his greatcoat. He was quiet. Gazing half into the darkening sky and half, I guess, into memory, he narrowed his eyes and I only just caught his words: 'Mortars – lots of them.'

*

The drive into Croatia was through a rolling, wintry landscape, through fields of uncut maize and past ice-rimed, leafless trees. It was an edgy drive: here was a building blown to pieces, here a pile of rubble marking where a house had been, here a car lying burned-out on its roof. There were tank-traps made of concrete blocks pinned through with steel bars, and the road was guarded by sandbag bunkers all the way. Heavily armed soldiers checked passing vehicles, while nervous civilians toted guns.

In the Lippizaner stud at Djakovo, Ivaca Mandic, the stud manager, and Branka Mioc of Ivandor delivered a serious warning. If there were any leaks to the press about an evacuation of horses, we would pay in blood. Our blood. This little warning was no idle threat. We were given it while we were gazing at a man lunging a stallion in the snow. In the distance was the peculiar shuffling sound of shellfire, and if any picture of that place and that moment will stick in my mind it is of that man and that stallion going round and round in the snow to the sound of distant explosions and the patter of machine-gun fire. I shivered.

Back in Harkany, I waited for the ILPH horsebox to make its way across Europe. Colonel George had returned to England by air. I waited anxiously in my hotel room until there came a knock on the door. I opened it. On the other side stood Jack Ritson. 'Evening,' he said. 'The bar's shut.' As if I didn't know.

Behind him were Norman Brown, ILPH field officer, Bob Westecott of the British Horse Society, and Ian Langstaff and Gavin Crowther of Martin Bird Productions, a film company.

We considered our options while we waited for instructions. The signals we were getting from the Croats were confusing. Did they want these horses out, or didn't they? Did they or did they not want to use our truck? We began to suspect that they did not want the horses evacuated at all, because in some curious way, the presence of the horses protected the town from Serbian bombardment. The place was rife with rumours, and I later discovered that there was a price on our heads – 400 Deutschmarks per capita, so to speak. But in any event there was a lot more to the Lippizaner affair than met the eye. There were complicated political ramifications.

And, in the end, the day before Christmas Eve 1991, the ILPH horsebox rolled back into the yard at Hall Farm – empty.

A month went by when suddenly a very peculiar request came to the ILPH from the Croatian Ministry of Agriculture in Zagreb. Would Colonel George Stephen choose a team to act as impartial observers at the exhumation of horses killed during the Serbian attack on the Lipik stud? For the second time we found ourselves on the battlefields of Croatia, this time in Lipik, at the stud itself.

It was a desperate sight. The land around was threaded with jumping-jack mines. The stud was blackened and roofless. Frost-whitened, bullet-holed trees stood, limbs hanging like the bones of shattered skeletons. The town was a shell. We drove through with an armed escort, out to the front lines, where the bodies of horses were being exhumed. Croatian pathologists were at hand: it was grisly work.

That day we heard the truth about what had happened at Lipik, and the attack on the stud had been just as sinister as we had supposed. Some of the horses had been ridden out at night by their grooms. Others had been herded out: many had died. Some had been transferred by the Croatian authorities to the comparative safety of Zagreb. But many had been stolen and found their way to Bosnia – which at this time had still not been engulfed in the war. We tried to trace them: we tried. We tried alongside the breed societies, and alongside the great kombinat of Ivandor, but it all remained shrouded in what George Stephen called 'the fog of war'.

In the university grounds of Zagreb, we found a few of the horses that had been rescued – a pitiful few.

And yet, with the supplies that had been sent out in that first truckful, and subsequent supplies from Lippizaner societies in England and Holland, the horses in Djakovo were safe – as safe as they could be, in the midst of war.

Of the horses in Bosnia? We heard only rumours.

The report that we were asked to write on the Lipik stud was accepted by the Croatians and became part of a larger report produced by the Faculty of Veterinary Medicine, University of Zagreb, entitled

'Animal Victims of Croatian Homeland War 1990–1992'. It makes for sorry reading. All kinds of animals were affected: cattle, pigs, dogs, horses, wildlife and those in the zoos of Sarajevo.

Some time after these events, I was in Abkhasya, in another war, a civil war, fought between the Abkhasyan and Georgian peoples. There, too, the sight of animals wandering helplessly round untended fields, hopelessly lost, was a tragic reminder of what we had seen in Croatia. One shudders to think of the potential ethnic problems surrounding the old Russian empire, and what there is yet to come.

Every war must in some way resemble another, the real victims being those who wanted no part of it, nor understood the reasons for it in the first place, nor had any defence against its appalling violence.

There is, in the aftermath of war, only silence.

Llanybyddyr is a market town in Wales lying about thirty-five miles due east of Cardigan and twelve miles south-west of Lampeter. It is small and the flavour agricultural, the surroundings hilly.

The Forestry Commission own land locally and have planted dark conifer forests here and there but everywhere else it is green.

This is rural Wales with its rural Welsh architecture and Celtic architecture is seldom pretty nowadays. This part of the country lies on the rim of the Cambrian Mountains, open to the westerlies and all the weather that comes with them, and can get up to sixty inches of rain a year. Accordingly, this is growing land, livestock land. Strong spring flushes of grass turn out animals fat and sleek and glossy.

These hills are known throughout the principality for sheep and cattle production but once were known for quality horses, and there was a time in Llanybyddyr market when you could expect to see 800 horses or more go under the hammer of a long morning's selling.

Today things are different.

When I went with Norman Brown we counted about 120 horses and ponies at the fair in total. Time of year affects numbers. The spring sale is the biggest, when the people who have survived the winter and wish to continue in business as trekking-centre owners come in to buy animals for the next summer season. That's when coloured horses and ponies fetch good money.

There were a few piebalds and skewbalds in the market when Norman and I walked in on that overcast day, when the first thing that wafted our way was the vinegary smell of fish and chips, fried onions and hot dogs, and the smooth scent of horses.

We walked down through the stalls, down through the saddlery and harness, boots, shoes, china and the bric-à-brac of the street fair, and the first horses we saw were a line of stallions.

Their owners had them in show harness, gleaming, oiled harness with the brass buckles polished and shining. And what a splendid sight they were!

The first in line was a 17.2hh Thoroughbred bay, who made the neat 16hh dapple grey beside him look small, while beside the grey a spotted Section A Welsh stallion pawed the ground and squealed.

Dwarfing the lot, peering into the distance, head high and ears pricked was a piebald Shire.

He was gazing away down through the stalls with his big black eyes, gazing through the people, through all the fuss and rattle and bang that madded about him, as, lost in a world of his own, he seemed to be looking at something privy to horses' eyes only, something humans could never see. The black across his back was shot through with an iridescent blue, like the back of a teal or a starling, and the white in the black was creamy. His feather had been all combed out, his tail was plaited, and flags were in his mane. He was no taller than the Thoroughbred, but his size and colour and presence gave him the advantage and as he gazed into the distance, his owner seemed to bask in his reflected glory.

That horse knew he was magnificent, even though by sheer comparison to the Thoroughbred his line was lumpy and neither fine nor aristocratic and in fact he couldn't hold a candle to that Thoroughbred for style. But he had something else you couldn't miss.

His keeper – it was almost impossible to think of him as his master – held him loosely on a headcollar and he didn't bother him at all. They were good buddies, you could see that. They knew each other, understood each other. Not an inch of fear for all that might and size: nothing but good old-fashioned horsemanship.

If that stallion had wanted to go I don't think a tractor could have held him. Yet he stood there, quietly beside his owner, gazing down through the stalls. Then he turned and came back to us, so to speak, nuzzled his keeper and blew softly through his great velvety nostrils sighing a huge sigh, as though we all bored him to death.

Norman Brown and I broke away and wandered off through the market.

Llanybyddyr had a reputation for being pretty rough a few years ago. It was a kind of charnel house for everything going. Regulations were thin on the ground then and those that existed were flouted or ignored, just as today when so many EC regulations are ignored on the Continent.

But that day, Llanybyddyr looked good. In the market proper I saw another Shire, a crossbred. He was a big, bony bay, an old horse. He had a saddle on and had been used in a riding school. He looked pretty dejected. His coat was rough – he hadn't been groomed for some time. Nobody cared much for him, that was clear. But he was a nice old horse with great big, sad eyes.

Norman looked at him, and ran a hand across his flanks. 'Poor old devil won't fetch much,' he said. 'Too old really, and big. Cost a fortune to keep.'

I looked back at his glossy piebald counterpart. What a contrast he was to this old fellow. How secure was his future. And how insecure was the future of this old horse and how his old eyes reflected it.

What fate would befall him, I wondered? What uncertainties lay ahead? I gazed at him for a moment, and saw Norman looking too.

To be sure, whether you are man or animal, there is no hell like uncertainty.

We left him and went round the rest of the stock.

In the market that day everyone knew Norman. And he told me about them: how a dealer will invariably split on another dealer, how such and such was a 'real rum beggar', how much this pony had fetched last time he saw her, where she'd come from, who owned her, what her name was, how many foals she'd had. It was an education.

He introduced me to welfare officers from the British Horse Society, The International Donkey Preservation Society, the RSPCA, someone from the Horse and Pony Protection Association. I met the Ministry of Agriculture vet and a few local charity people interested in horse welfare as well.

And as we walked past the charity stalls and the chip-eating people picking through the saddlery stores, riders walked or trotted past us, trying the paces of their newly acquired purchases, all done up with their plaited tails and oiled hooves.

I watched a girl groom a chestnut gelding she'd just bought or perhaps was selling. She was a pretty girl and lost in her work.

I watched a child scramble on to some favourite never-to-be-sold old jade.

And all the colour and variety of the day prompted me to reflect on the fact that we owe these organizations, these equine welfare charities, enormous debts of thanks and of recognition, the great and the small, because without them, places like Llanybyddyr could still easily be the rough places they once were.

Of course, charities have their disagreements. They have had their rivalries and battles with each other at executive level, they have had their jealousies. But there in Llanybyddyr they were all working together to ensure that nothing, literally nothing, slipped through the net.

Thanks to them my old Shire cross standing in the stalls would never have to face a sea journey.

I saw him sold later.

I couldn't see who had bid for him, but after the auctioneer's gavel hit its mark, I sought out his buyer.

'Your horse?' I asked.

'Yes!' replied a young woman. She was very pleased with her new acquisition.

'What's he going to be doing?'

'Oh, maybe a bit of harrowing ... and ...' she shouted over her shoulder as she walked him off to a waiting horsebox.

'And?' I queried as the old horse stepped up the ramp.

'He'll be a chum to my show-jumper.'

So that old nag was off to crop clover and pull a harrow in the green mountain where he grew up.

Had she not bought him, he might have wound up in a slaughter-house – who knows.

But he wouldn't have been shipped to an Italian one.

Leaving behind us the snows of Popocatapetl and Ixtaccihuatl rising above the grey-brown smog of Mexico City; leaving behind us the blue of the jacaranda and red flame trees, the mimosa and fran-gipani, we drove into the high Altiplano, where the trees were pine and the roadside vegetation sisal and lantana. The air became cooler and Mexico City behind us seemed sweat-rimed and suffocating.

We drove on up out of the trees and on to a long plain, where the houses were single-storey breeze-block places: shanty towns with iron reinforcing rods sticking up above unfinished roofs, like the houses of North Africa, and for the same reason: there's no tax levied on an unfinished construction in either place.

This was dirt farming land with *burros* and horses out in the fields drilling corn. Horse-riding country, where men and draught animals graft and sweat and women and children pound grain into tortillas, where the men swig *pulque* and the markets are hard, tight-fisted places where the bargaining is sharp and deals made fast.

We swung along the road in a kind of a muzzy silence, passing the huge sombreroed statue of Emiliano Zapata, Mexican hero cast in bronze, sitting on his horse high above the trees, rifle in hand, bandoliers across his chest, gazing out hollow-eyed over the country that he freed.

Off the main road a small river wound along a narrow valley bor-dered by willow and carob trees, and a hundred yards or more beyond it a line of trucks glittered in the sun: the market of St Bernabe.

We drove up into it and sat tight.

We were worried because we'd been told that the word was out that a group of foreigners would be arriving to make a film, and the buzz was not to make them any too welcome.

We waited. What for I'm not certain.

But when no one seemed interested in us, we climbed out of our combi-wagon, and took a look around.

The market itself lay in a kind of buckle of ground, with all the market traders' tents pitched at angles on one slope and all the trucks on the opposite slope backed up against a rough earth bank which had been cut away so the animals they carried had somewhere to jump out on to. That bank had been cut courtesy of IDPT and ILPH money. Before that the animals had been whacked out of the back of the trucks down on to the ground, and that's a long way for slender legs.

From the traders' tents came the scents of tortillas burning and meat singeing, the sticky smell of freshly tanned leather, and the whiff of dung. Music thumped ceaselessly, drowned occasionally by a fellow giving us the rundown on sheep prices, bawling into a loudspeaker right beside us.

Way above it all, in the distance aloof and clean, hung the peak of Toluca volcano, with its rivers of snow lying like white hair over the shoulders of some ancient and dignified god gazing down from afar in mighty and silent resignation.

Moving through the trucks and over broken ground we stood over the market and watched.

Animals were being unloaded from trucks, tied to fenders and makeshift tethering posts. The place was full of people wandering through them, sizing up this one, feeling the muscle or flank of that one.

Sarah Bligh and Alastair Martin-Bird of the film crew went off to find the shots, leaving Ian Langstaff and Mark Jennings with the camera and sound kit. I joined them as they set up the camera and took it down again, filmed this, got an angle on that.

Among the first animals Ian filmed was a yearling filly with a broken hock: Tina MacGregor had patched her up as best she could before we got there, but time was running out for that little filly. In an English market she wouldn't have been passed fit to be sold in the first place, or she'd have been put down on the spot. But economics dictate in St Bernabe and there's not a lot of room for sentiment, so she had to wait all day to be loaded back on to the truck at sunset before she could be put down.

Beside the filly a donkey had collapsed. The ILPH vets

pronounced her beyond help and amazingly, her owner gave them permission to put her out of her misery without further ado. One quick shot with a humane killer and she was gone.

And all round us men were tugging and whacking horses and mules, whooping them along in strings, or tossing stones to drive them; bewildered, frightened animals weaved this way and that driven by owners trying to make a hand's turn on the day's trading.

Squatting down there in among the dirt and the sweat filming all this were Ian Langstaff and Mark Jennings. They filmed the WTFE farriers and the IDPT and ILPH vets. They filmed the whole thing.

The high dome of the church rises above the market place of Capulhuac, Mexico, where the wood lay about in heaps. Each pile must have weighed getting on for 100 kilos.

The market itself is long. One side is bordered by a two-storey galleried building running off a side portico of the church: the other by town houses, simple little single-storey places and pretty mean at that.

Women were bartering the wood for whatever they could get for it – anything from dollops of lard, to clothes, to pineapples, vegetables, saucepans, blankets, shirts, chickens and avocados. No money was involved. Capulhuac is a barterer's market.

As the morning wore on, more and more horses, donkeys and mules came in with their loads of wood. Some were so exhausted that they just stood swaying, waiting for the wood to be unstrung and swung off their backs.

It was difficult to say how far they'd walked in that heat. Some of the loads were a lot bigger than the donkeys and the only thing they had to cover their backs was hessian sacking and blankets, which made them hotter still, so that the sweat underneath rumpled the skin, and the backs of some of the animals when Carlos and Tina pulled the packs off were raw.

A couple of old men had turned up with a big can full of *pulque*, as they call it locally, a drink made from agave. It's a white liquor and these fellows were swilling it like beer, pouring the stuff into plastic mugs on the street corners. One or two were well gone, staggering round and singing, while their women haggled and bartered and the horses stood in the sun, tethered to odd bits of iron rod poking out of some part-built shack.

It was an airless place.

Ian Langstaff moved his camera to the open ground of the market, facing directly into the sun. You could see where it had burned him the day before and his forehead was red and blistered. Mark Jennings the sound man had heat stroke: he looked pretty sick. But he caught the sounds anyway and Ian caught the shots and Alastair Martin-Bird looked nervously for new locations, new ways to express on film what was happening here.

Everyone sweltered, both horses and men.

I watched Walt sweating as he shod a mule.

Nearby, under the shade of a walnut tree, the horses had a moment's respite while the farriers trimmed their feet and we – the foreigners, the film crew – distributed water and lucerne. The vets pulled the packs off the horses' backs and did what they could for the worst injuries by making poultices of cloth into doughnut rings and placing them under the packs so they didn't rub any more, and the horses could carry their loads without pain. I don't know how much of their work went noticed. Too much *pulque* had been drunk. But I saw one or two take things in. One or two is how things start.

Apparently all the wood sold in Capulhuac is cut illegally, so you are forced to wonder whether what you are doing is right. If you give them a hand to improve their horses, does that mean they'll hack down more forest to sell more wood? And if they don't hack it down how are they going to live anyway? How are they going to get their food and clothes, their avocados and *pulque*?

And if you don't lend a hand, do you just stand by and watch the donkeys and the mules get worn to nothing? Do you stand by and let the maggots eat them under their packs?

Mohammed the Stick rides his bike fifteen kilometres to the souk to shoe the horses, and that's on Tuesdays. On the other days he works under the palm trees where the *calèches* line up, below the Koutoubia, where the Imam calls the faithful to prayer, beside the medina, in Marrakesh, Morocco.

A year before, Mohammed had been hustling round for work on his bike, making a thin living from shoeing horses with half round shoes with calkins. Now he shoes them flat.

He does from ten to twelve horses a day and he shoes them with open heels, just like Walt showed him.

About two hours' drive south of Marrakesh lies the village of Ourika, where Souk L'Etnin, a street market, is held every Tuesday. The souk stands on the far side of a long low stone bridge which spans a wide, smooth-bouldered watercourse that at first I thought was dry. In fact, in the middle ran a small fast river which rose in the smoky blue of the mountains behind.

On market days the people tether their donkeys and mules in lines down on the river bed, while the more thoughtful lead theirs beneath the arches of the bridge so they can be in shade. There the animals wait for their owners to sell whatever they have brought before plodding home on the long winding tracks into the mountains.

When we got there the day's trading was already in full swing although it was barely eight in the morning. Sheep, tied by the feet, bleated as they were bartered. Chickens, tied by the feet and hanging over donkeys' backs, panted in the sun and mules dozed, heads down, in silence. Old men, white-bearded and straw-hatted, walked slowly through the crowds, dressed in their coloured and striped djellabas, like something out of the illustrations in a children's Bible. Brightly dressed water-bearers, all decked out in reds and purples and wearing their big, coloured hats with their pom-pom fringes, went round ringing bells and carrying goatskins full of water for a coin a swig which you got from a little brass bowl. Past the souk was Ourika, the village, with its crenellated mosque and pink-sand-coloured houses with jacaranda blueing the walls, and hibiscus growing in bright scarlet clumps. Behind the village were groves of olives and behind the olives, shrouded in early morning haze and heat, shimmered the Atlas, where the river rose. You could just make out the valleys: huge, deep, green valleys lined with terraces. There were settlements right up on the mountain and brittle stone-dry patches on the south side where the sun hit hard and no vegetation grew. You could smell the mountains too – a dry curry-spice, herby scent that filled the market.

The market itself was decked in soft and natural colours and there was a striking absence of plastics. In the low fawn canvas tents were herbs for sale, and spices laid out on display providing a smooth, even tone, rich in deep reds, and indigos, saffrons and kohl. Under the noise of the market – the bartering, the animals and the shouting – was the soft rippling sound of the river.

On their haunches down beside the flood bank, a group of farriers were banging away at their pin anvils, whacking shoes on the donkeys and mules that were brought to them, and in the back of the souk people were cooking, grilling fish which they served with chillies and a whang of bread; or chunks of meat freshly killed and grilled with tomato. You could buy a bite and squat down with the old men and eat under the shade of gums and carobs and watch the people in the souk, down by the river, or watch the farriers shoe the horses and the mules.

Alastair called over to Ian Langstaff. 'Get the shot?'

The huge souk at Ben Guerir was another matter altogether.

This roasting, airless, heaving place was filled with such a press of humans and animals you began to wonder if there was any chance of anyone getting anywhere, or if the whole souk would seize up somehow and come grinding to a sweating, swearing halt. The thoroughfare, such as it was, through the middle was packed with piles of vegetables, onions and courgettes, heaps of spices, and collections of galvanized buckets and string and rope and tent pegs slammed into the ground pulling tent ropes tight so that people tripped over them and fruit rolled out of their baskets. And the donkey carts got wedged together and people were shouting and flies were buzzing and in among all this was the Family Planning truck playing some piece of music which did nothing to draw the crowds away from Ian Langstaff and his camera, as he struggled in the press of people to film one of the farriers – Ali Bardoud – showing another old boy a different, better way.

Whipping through the sleet and the drumming dark night wind, Jacques Le Marquis kept his beat-up old Mercedes tucked in the nearside lane behind the Italian horse transporter to the border at Český Těšín between Poland and Czechoslovakia. He logged the time it took to clear the crossing and when the truck passed through he kept pace behind it along the cold windswept road through the Tatra Mountains to Zelina, all the way down to the Hungarian border. He'd been driving all day and all night and had managed to get alongside the truck enough times to see there were horses illegally loaded, stacked in double tiers inside it.

Out in his car in the rain he timed the drivers as they went into the border café for a coffee. Three hours they were there, and while he waited he checked the horses in the truck.

Cold, wet, hungry, thirsty Polish horses.

He logged his information. He logged the time, the registration number of the truck and the approximate distance covered.

By the time the drivers came out of the café the sleet had turned to snow. As the truck started, Jacques followed it down through Hungary to the border crossing into Romania, where he waited with the horses as the drivers disappeared again for another six hours, until they came out of a hotel having had something resembling sleep. When they checked through customs he was waiting and when they hit the road he was on their tail, and he followed them through Slavonia to Italy where the horses were unloaded. He counted them off and made a note of it. He'd made a note of everything.

Pitching through the sea of the South Atlantic, Jean Peloux was in the lowest hold with the horses where the temperature was over 100° Fahrenheit. One of the fans in the stern had packed up and a dozen horses were nearly being boiled alive. But Jean was in there with two Filipino engineers, and he made them graft until that fan was going again. He made three others fetch water and he made them sponge the horses.

'But, señor, they are condemned! They will die anyway!'

'Not as long as they are on this boat with me!'

As the day wore on the wind blew up, a bitter, strong South Atlantic wind that whipped up the sea. Soon the blue turned to grey and the ship began to heave. Some of the horses started to bite, to fight, to try to kick each other, but Jean was there to run his hand over frightened backs.

'*Taisez-vous, mes petits!*' he said.

He got the crew to feed more lucerne – eating to a horse is like milk to a baby or like whisky to a Scotsman.

He walked up to the first deck of horses – 400 of them. Then he cut down the steel ramp that leads to the second deck, the second hold, past rust-rimmed rails and fire hoses, through the scent of fresh paint and salt water down into the bowels of the ship, into the scent of oil and fear, dung and urine.

Here the horses were restless. They had been frightened by the deep throbbing sound of the ship's engines and the sudden shudders as the propellors lost grip in the water. Jean smoothed away their fear, and talked to them, all 400 of them. Then he went lower still.

The headroom here had shrunk to a mere few feet. One of the Criollos had cut its eyes on a sharp piece of ducting overhead. Jean had the ducting bound in cloth and the horse treated but he'd been blinded. He watched as another horse came to stand beside the duct and wasn't surprised to see the same horse remain beside it for the next three weeks at sea.

He went down to the lowest deck, an uneven place dingy with cobwebbed lights and the smell of diesel and fish, tar and sweat, which boomed with the noise of the sea, the moan of the fans and the whirr of electric motors. Feed had been scattered any old how among the horses' feet. He called one of the crew to feed them properly.

'But señor, these are condemned horses. They are going to die!'

'Right now they are fit, hungry, thirsty and frightened and as long as I'm on this ship they're going to live!'

Jean didn't go up on deck to be in the fresh air, away from the smell and the horses. He stayed with them, in the gloom, all 1600 of them, whispering them a little peace, a little calm in the storm that roared about them.

Looking down on a thin grey mare lying in a shallow pit, Dr Menache, ILPH Inspector for Israel, took a needle out of his bag. Over his head the sun was high and hot and in the shimmering distance, through the olive trees, glinted the Dead Sea.

The mare, he guessed, was about six years old. She was little more than a skeleton. He reckoned she must have fallen into the pit about three days before; he could see where she had struggled to get up.

Dr Menache held the needle up to the sun and inverted a small bottle. Then he walked down to the mare. Her eyes were already glazed over, her breathing weak and ragged. Her lower lip drooped. The needle went in and she shuddered. He walked back to the truck and made his notes: 'Abandoned mare; fatal dose administered at 12.15 p.m.'

He put the pen down, closed his notebook. He'd make arrangements to have the horse removed. He checked his schedule for the rest of the day. 'Nazareth – stray mules seen near dump. Investigate.' Casting a last look back at the dead mare, he fired up the engine and drove away.

André Bubear bent down and took a pair of steel pliers from the array of tools at his feet, and turning to the old horse beside him gently began to cut the wire noseband which had become embedded in the skin across the horse's muzzle.

'*Mashallah!*' A man beside him gagged, and turned away.

André snipped the wire. The headpiece fell free. Tina MacGregor was ready with a needle and disinfectant.

'It's OK: we can get this without drastic surgery. The infection's not too bad.'

André snipped again. The wire came free. Tina teased it across the nasal passage. By its constant movement the wire had made a hole in the skin right across the bridge of the horse's nose. Without causing major contusion, Tina slid it out.

'Poor sod,' André said, as Tina cleaned the wound.

'This horse has to work today. He could really do with a rest.'

But this was Jordan and the horse's owner needed him. That's the price of life close to the bone.

'It's OK,' André said, 'I'll make him a wide enough noseband; it'll just be a bit high, that's all.'

And he took a piece of webbing and measured and cut and fashioned a headcollar and fitted it.

The horse's owner thanked him and André watched as he took the horse away through the sun-browned buildings, past the army trucks and out into the blistering heat of the desert beyond.

'Right,' he said, turning round, 'Take the harness off that old mule: let's see what we can do.'

On the other side of the world, Beth McFarlane, Administrator of ILPH New Zealand, marshalled her statistics and her evidence as she prepared for the next round in the battle to prevent the culling of her country's feral horse population by shooting.

And in the International Departure lounge of Johannesburg Airport, Colonel George Stephen shook hands with Ken Palmer, Chairman of the National Thoroughbred Trust of South Africa. It had been a fruitful meeting. Reviving a sixty-year-old link with South Africa, the Chief Executive of the ILPH had been impressed with the dedication the members of the National Thoroughbred Trust had shown to their work, to secure for old racehorses a future free from exploitation, misuse or neglect. In that handshake there was both the recognition of a bond shared and the promise of future collaboration.

Wherever in the world the ILPH is working, all relevant material gathered is sent back to its headquarters at Hall Farm, where it goes through the system.

Where issues are at stake, questions are asked.

What exactly is the nature of the problem? Does it need instant redress? Is it a practical or political issue? Are funds needed? Is it a question of help, or a question of further investigation? Does it need expert attention? Is it an issue of abuse and could it involve the ILPH in legal proceedings? Is there a precedent? And finally, and most importantly, if everything else seems in order, would ILPH members back it?

Once the information has gone through this process it is submitted for Council approval and if that is sanctioned then action follows.

If it is a big single issue involving huge funds – as was the 1992 minimum values crisis which took up a quarter of a million – then a campaign is launched by the PR team and depending on what type of issue it is that campaign will be targeted accordingly.

During the summer you might see Liz Hatton driving round the shows in the big green ILPH horsebox. She'll be exhibiting for the ILPH: she's the public face that tells the ILPH story; what it's all about, who's who and where it's working. She hands out leaflets and sells videos, books, and items from the ILPH catalogue. She calls herself the ILPH Exhibitionist.

Liz has contact with the most important part of the ILPH: its members.

ILPH members gave it life in the first place. Its members helped it grow and nourished it when the going was tough. They supported it through the briars of opposition and helped to pave the way for legislation by their cumulative support. They pushed when they were asked – sometimes unasked – and dug deep in their pockets when money was needed.

Those members come from all walks of life, and from all parts of the country; and if they confronted each other they might disagree – some might be supporters of hunting while others oppose it – and so it is in the ILPH office: that is how the world works in reality. But they are united for the common good of the horse and see past their divisions and differences in pursuit of their shared goal.

It is only with the help of its members that the ILPH can respond in the way it does to crises in any part of the world, and there are few countries where it has not worked at some time – as I write there's an ILPH man in deepest China.

And if its staff are the structure and the skeleton that make up the ILPH, then its members are the blood and muscle that ultimately provide the energy with which things happen.

Through them have come all manner of things, from cash donations to land, from gifts to legacies, from the two pounds per week sent by two old ladies in a flat in London, or a few pence from schoolchildren, to tens of thousands given anonymously and out of the blue.

Donations come in a passive sense, too – members of staff who don't claim expenses or who cover bills that are rightly not theirs. All these things are statements of support and confidence. They are a trust.

And some of the members are old indeed. Recently a letter arrived from Chris Smith, a real old international horseman:

It gives me great pleasure to enclose a cheque for £50 for life membership of the ILPH in memory of my Injun-trained pony Mary, on whose back I rode ten miles to school and back in the summer of 1918 across featureless prairie in Alberta, 20 miles south of the railhead at Manyberries.

I was born in June 1911 and 1912 found me with my parents on a happy mission station at Beighien near the mouth of the Yangtze Kiang, Shanting, northern China. Here, there was a donkey on which Chee-Sin-Ee, our Chinese cook, used to take my kid brother and me for rides, he in a pannier on one side balanced by a pannier of stones on t'other while I rode atop chocked off by the panniers.

Sadly the donkey died of tetanus before we left in 1917...

Now to Mary.

She was quite a character, black all over except for a white face on one side with a black eye and a white blind eye on the other black side. She was not a beauty. Archie Witnick had a grin on his face when he brought her over and a bigger grin some days later when he brought her back after she snatched the halter out of my seven-year-old hand and bolted home . . . but eventually I learned to ride her.

Archie had warned us 'Never tie her up or she'll go mad. Chuck the reins over her head and she'll graze peaceable like.' That's the way the Injuns do it.

Well, in the spring of 1919 we couldn't catch Mary . . . but eventually we cornered her and I rode her once more and on coming home, I forgot the rules. I tied her up.

I was just eating my bacon and eggs – sunny side up of course – when there was the sound of thunder in a clear blue sky. We looked out and saw the barn shaking . . .

And he tells us how his pa had to tackle the mad Mary, how his mother had to cut the halter rope and how the dust didn't settle for days. Then he goes on:

'Why am I writing all this to you? Well, I understand horses are your business so I thought you might be kind enough to me to read my dotage reminiscences. Assuming I am to be a life member it looks like you might be lumbered with me, but . . .' and he adds finally, 'it's just a great joy . . .' Here is another, shorter letter from a little girl seventy-six years his junior:

Please stop the poor horses on ships. Please stop the men being hurty to them.

In those simple words lies the point of this story.

In Chris Smith's letter, its spirit.

Ada Cole once said that she wished she could see her work continue. She added that it 'must go on to the end'.

Without Anne Colvin's fortitude and determination, no doubt all of Ada Cole's efforts would have been in vain. She has now passed on that obligation and the ILPH works with greater dynamic today than it has ever done.

The resolve to fulfil its commitments in Britain and overseas is powerfully charged. The ILPH will work with any charity or organization which has similar aims in order to achieve these ends. From it sprang the Ada Cole Memorial Stables. Mona Huskie, who founded the Horse and Pony Protection Association, first worked for the ILPH. It was a founder member of the World Society for the Protection of Animals. Dorothy Brooke was able to sustain her Cairo Hospital because of it, and now the LLuest Trust looks to it for its continuing aid. World Training for Equines is able to work through it and the World Farriers Association can call upon it for support, as does the Animal Health Trust, The Royal Veterinary School and those who benefit from its scholarships.

In the field the work goes on. And sometimes, the sight of animals suffering moves you not to tears, nor anger, nor indignation but simply to a sense of overwhelming futility. What is the point? Who will listen? And even if you show people another, better way to treat their horses, can you be sure they will do what you ask when your back is turned? But you know you must not think like that. You know that you can only look forward, and that your reach should outstretch your grasp.

Perhaps after all there will never be a time when horses, and their fellow equines, are strangers to pain.

But if the vision of such a future – a future free from pain and fear – is ever to be realized, it will come about because of the spirit of all those who have worked in the ILPH and their desire to see good husbandry carried to every corner of the world. And it will come about because of those people who acknowledged the debt they were charged with, and honoured it.

If all these animals could cry aloud with
one voice, it would stir the world to do
something about it all. One of the most dreadful
things about this traffic is that thousands
of horses go to doom and agony, trudging along
willingly and trustfully and in mute silence.
We must be their voice.

ADA COLE, 1927

The Story of the ILPH:
Step by Step

1911	Ada Cole sees heavy horses being disembarked at Antwerp
1914	Exportation of Horses Act, as a corollary to the Diseases of Animals Act 1894, makes it illegal to transport animals unfit to travel. It names five ports only to be used for export of horses
1914	Ada Cole joins her sister in a convent at Nimes, Belgium, and First World War breaks out
1917	Both are imprisoned for complicity and, ultimately, spying
1918	Armistice; Ada Cole and her sister are released
1919	Ada Cole is decorated for helping patriots escape during the war by the King of Belgium, who also commends and awards her a citation for bravery
1919	She returns to England
1920	She sees horses being exported again from King's Lynn
1920–3	Travels with the horses to Vaugirard Abattoir in Paris
1924–5	Old Horse Traffic Committee formed
1927	Sadie Baum (Anne Colvin) employed as secretary
1927	Mona Huskie and Dr Rose Turner accompany horses to Vaugirard Abattoir
1927	International League Against the Export of Horses for Butchery founded

1928   Ada Cole invited to sit on RSPCA Council

1929   Klondike Abattoir established, Bourne, Lincolnshire, to be run as a model slaughterhouse

1930   Dorothy Brooke introduces Geoffrey Gilbey to Ada Cole

1930   Geoffrey Gilbey's exposure of the atrocities at Vaugirard Abattoir confirms Ada Cole's work

1930   On 17 October, Ada Cole dies

1930   Geoffrey Gilbey becomes first Chairman of ILaEHB

1931   Brigadier General Sir George Cockerill resigns seat in Parliament, is taken on as joint Honorary Director and submits his first Exportation of Horses Bill, which fails to be read

1932   Brigadier General Sir George Cockerill draws up the first Draft Convention to protect animals transported by land and sea from preventable suffering

1932   Ada Cole Memorial Stables opened by Her Grace The Duchess of Hamilton, in South Mimms

1932   Investigations of shipments of slaughter horses from Canada result in a cessation of the trade (temporarily)

1933   Freddy Fox speaks at the Eccentric Club of the horrors of live horses for slaughter and joins ILaEHB as an influential supporter

1934   Yorkshire Branch, first of the independent branches of the ILaEHB opened in Yorkshire by Miss Tope

1934   Dorothy Brooke (of the Brooke Hospital) sits on the ILaEHB Council

1937   The Exportation of Horses Act, drafted by Sir George Cockerill, establishes the principle of Minimum Values, receives Royal Assent on 1 October

1937   National Council Against the Export of Horses for Butchery amalgamates with ILaEHB and the new name of the International League for the Protection of Horses is first coined

1937   Southern Counties Branch opened

1939   Riding Establishments Act, drafted in consultation with the ILPH

1939   Major-General Geoffrey Brooke joins the ILPH Council

1939–45 War years. ILPH branches buy up old and worn horses by the thousand

1939   Freddy Fox killed in a car accident

1948   Cherry Tree Farm bought

1950   The Exportation of Horses Act (Minimum Values Order) brought about as a result of ILPH evidence submitted to Lord Rosebery's Committee of Enquiry into the export and slaughter of horses

1950   Mark Colvin addresses the World Congress for Animal Protection held in The Hague, August 1950, and obtains an insertion in the International Convention of a clause securing to all animals effective protection during transport, which was unanimously endorsed

1950   Diseases of Animals Act incorporated the values of The Exportation of Horses (Minimum Values) 1950 Order and consolidated all previous Acts. In exercise of the powers vested in him by this Act the Minister of Agriculture issued the following Order:

1951   The Transit of Horses Order, which was designed to protect horses during carriage by road and rail

1952   Deed of Trust Declaration drawn up

1952   Horses (Sea Transport) Order 1952, which dealt with the conditions of horses transported at sea

1953   Alkrington Home of Rest for Horses, Manchester, opened

1954   The Slaughter of Animals (Amendment) Act, which implemented recommendations of the Duke of Northumberland's Committee into the slaughter of horses

1954   Slaughter of Animals (Prevention of Cruelty) No. 2 Regulation, which secured humane conditions and practices in connection with the slaughter of animals

1954   Horses (Landing from Northern Ireland and the Republic of Ireland) Order, which protected horses imported into Great Britain from suffering on landing and in transit after landing

1955   Anne Colvin receives the MBE for services to equine welfare

1955   Patrick Keatley, friend of Ada Cole and distinguished journalist, receives commendation as Journalist of Honour for work done for the welfare of animals transported by land and sea

1955   Dorothy Brooke dies in Cairo

1955   Formal Association with Klondike Abattoir ends

1957   Sir George Cockerill dies

1957   Herr Von Braunbehrens of Germany dies, and the German office disappears

1957   Lt. Col. Sir Thomas Moore, BART, CBE, MP becomes third Chairman of the ILPH

1958   Slaughterhouses Act, information for which law was collated by the field officers of the ILPH

1959   ILPH exposed the *City of Waterford* disaster which concerned a shipment of horses from Ireland to the Continent

1960   Henry Payne becomes fourth Chairman of the ILPH Council, Kay Colvin becomes Director

1960   ILPH buys Stepaside Farm, Dublin

1961   First ILPH Scholarship awarded to Alexander Littlejohn of Natal, South Africa

1961   Death of Harry Hardaker, first manager of Cherry Tree Farm

1962   Overa House Farm loaned by Captain Bennington to the ILPH as a home of rest

1962   Captain Charles Bennington becomes Honorary Field Supervisor for the ILPH

1962   ILPH inaugurates its stables in Seville, Spain

1962   ILPH with the RSPCA donate two horseboxes and trailers to fledgling equine welfare establishments in Athens

1962   Little Church Farm, Wilstead, Bedfordshire, bought and run by Mr Sawkins

1964   Riding Establishments Act

1969   Sir Robert Cary's Ponies Act prescribes a Minimum Value for a pony to close the loophole in the law which previous legislation had left untackled. This Minimum Value had to be certified by an accredited valuer. Sir Robert Cary was at the time patron of the ILPH

1971   Lady Grey Egerton Home of Rest for Horses set up in Sidlesham, Chichester

1971   Wheal Ellen Home, Cornwall, leased to the ILPH

1971   Kay Colvin retires as Director

1972   Captain Charles Bennington becomes Honorary Director

1974   Lady Grey Home closes

1974   Wheal Ellen home withdrawn

1974   ILPH worth its first million

1974   Links with Spain cut owing to heavy increase in cost

1975   Roger Macchia engaged as Inspector General in Europe

1978   Minimum Values Order

1980   Eurogroup formed

1987   Hall Farm, Snetterton, bought

1988   Norman McLeod joins Council

1988   Norman McLeod becomes Chairman of Council

1988   Colonel George McL Stephen becomes the ILPH's first Chief Executive

1988   Colonel Richard Felton becomes first General Manager

1988   The Great Step Forward

1990   New office block built in Snetterton

1990   Relocation of offices from London to Norfolk

1990   Computerization of office records, details etc.

1990   The Welfare of Horses at Markets (and other places of sale) Order, enforced as from 1 March 1991

1991   Stepaside Farm sold

1991   Retention of Minimum Values Order

1992   Captain Charles Bennington dies

1992   Anne Colvin dies

1992   Working Together for Equines programme taken on indefinitely

1992   Sarah Bligh and Alastair Martin-Bird produce the first ILPH corporate video

1993   Philip Billington becomes Chairman

1994   HRH The Princess Royal becomes president

APPENDIX 2

Declaration of Trust Deed:
Third Schedule

Objects of the ILPH

The ILPH exists for the world-wide protection and rehabilitation of horses. This is achieved through:

1. Rescuing and rehabilitating equines found to be at risk.

2. The establishment of equine Rest and Rehabilitation Centres in the United Kingdom and overseas.

3. The placement on loan, under ILPH supervision, of rehabilitated equines in suitable homes.

4. Providing a final retirement home at its centres for a limited number of equines.

5. The investigation of all complaints of cruelty and neglect involving equines and, where appropriate, taking action to prevent further suffering and abuse to these equines.

6. The monitoring of ports, horse sales, markets and riding schools to ensure that equines are properly transported, stabled, fed and handled in accordance with the principles of good equine management and the statutory provisions governing their welfare.

7. The monitoring of establishments for the disposal of equines, such as abattoirs and knackers' yards, to ensure that adequate facilities are available, and that these provide humane, practical, and where necessary, affordable methods of disposal.

8. The sponsorship or active support of all legislation to further equine care.

9. The making of representations to the appropriate authorities and the organization of campaigns to ensure the safety and well-being of equines.

10. Collaboration with other charities or organizations who have a mutual interest in the welfare of equines or whose work is closely connected with equines.

11. Providing education on equine welfare matters so as to reduce cruelty through ignorance.

12. Sponsoring scholarship and projects connected with equine care.

13. The establishment overseas of branches of the ILPH to further the objects of the ILPH.

14. The use of the media and other methods to promote the objects of the ILPH.

15. The use of ILPH funds to finance activities, projects and the provision of financial assistance, in pursuance of the objects of the ILPH.

16. The generation of income to support the activities of the ILPH in pursuance of the objects of the ILPH.

INDEX